LATIN GLORY

LATIN GLORY

Airlines of Latin America

MICHAEL MAGNUSSON

Airlife
England

AUTHOR'S NOTE

This book is the result of twenty years collecting and photographing airliners in Latin America and the Caribbean. Michael Magnusson has lived for five years in Argentina, and subsequently travelled extensively in the area as an aircraft salesman which has given him many opportunities to photograph rare and interesting aircraft. All photographs have been taken with Konica and Nikon cameras using K25 & K64 Kodachrome film. Unless otherwise indicated, all photos were taken by the author.

The information about the various airlines has been taken from the following sources: *Air Transport World*, *Airlines of Latin America* (R.E.G.Davies), *Air Britain* (various publications), *Aviation Letter*, *JP Airline Fleets* and the author's own notes. For any reader who wants more historical information about the airlines featured, the author strongly recommends R.E.G.Davies' book on *Airlines of Latin America*, published by Putnam in 1984.

To fill some gaps in the coverage, the author has also used photographs taken by the following photographers: Aerogem, Eddy Gual (Aviation Photography of Miami), Tony Härry, Dan Hagedorn, Tommy Lakmaker and Jean-M. Magendie.

Copyright © 1995 by Michael Magnusson

First published in the UK in 1995
by Airlife Publishing Ltd.

British Library Cataloguing in Publication Data
A catalogue record for this book
is available from the British Library

ISBN 1 85310 431 0

Printed in Singapore by Kyodo Printing Co. (S'pore) Pte Ltd.

Airlife Publishing Ltd.

101 Longden Road, Shrewsbury SY3 9EB

CONTENTS

ARGENTINA

AEROLINEAS ARGENTINAS

This company was formed on 5thMay, 1949, out of the merger of four carriers, ALFA, Aeroposta, FAMA and Zonda. Its initial fleet was a great mix of types but it soon settled down for the DC-3s, DC-4s, DC-6s, CV-240s and Shorts Sandringhams. In 1950 Aerolineas relaunched the services to New York and Europe that were previously operated by FAMA. It became one of the first jet operators in South America when it introduced the DH Comet in 1959. This was soon followed by orders for three Caravelles and nine Avro 748s in 1961. Aerolineas retired its DC-3s in 1966-67 by transferring these and some routes to LADE, incidentally the same year saw the phase-out of the DC-6s as well. The DC-4s soldiered on until 1970 when finally replaced by brand new B-737s. The CV-240s having been sold in 1962 to the newly started LAP in Paraguay. To replace the Comets on the long-haul routes Aerolineas ordered four new B-707s in September 1965. It eventually built up a fleet of eight. The next type to be ordered was the B737 in 1970 when Aerolineas ordered six, and thus it could finally retire the DH Comets. The B737s were good for the domestic trunk routes but Aerolineas still needed a replacement for the 748s. It finally chose the F28-1000, three being ordered in November 1974, and when they were delivered the following year they introduced Aerolineas current livery, replacing the previous blue-cheatline.

Later B727-200s and B747s arrived so that by 1990 Aerolineas fleet consisted of six B747-200s, one B747SP, one B707, eight B727-200s, eleven B737-200s and three F28s.

Meanwhile Aerolineas was privatized, and sold to Iberia in partnership with "Cielos del Sur", the new owner of Austral. The fleet remains the same except the B707 and B747SP are gone, instead Aerolineas have started taking delivery of new MD-88s originally ordered by Austral.

B-737 caught in the old livery at Aeroparque airport in July 1974. The 737 was the only type to feature this livery, all other aircraft had a simple blue cheatline with the stylized condor on the fin.

AER

Aerotransportes Entre Rios was founded in 1962 as an all-cargo carrier specializing in carrying livestock within South America. Initial equipment was C-46s. However, an ex-KLM L-749 Constellation joined the fleet in 1964, and this was followed by four L-1049s. By this time AER was a regular visitor to Miami. The piston aircraft were replaced by turbine equipment in the early 1970s when a single Britannia and various CC-106s were put into service. However these were not happy times for AER, as it rapidly lost both the Britannia and then two CC-106s in accidents. By the mid-1970s only two CC-106s remained in service and the airline started reducing its operations. After one was sold in 1978 to Uruguay the other ended up stored at Ezeiza airport.

CC-106 LV-JZB caught during one of its regular visits to Miami in 1977. (ALPS). The following year it went to ALAS in Uruguay, but only lasted one year until it was damaged beyond repair during a hard landing in Montevideo.

ALFA (AEROCHACO)

Aerochaco was founded in 1957 by the Chaco province in northern Argentina, and it began services two years later with a single DH Beaver. Once a second Beaver joined the fleet, the network was expanded in the early 1960s from Resistencia, its home base. In 1968 Aerochaco acquired three new Twin Otters and continued its gradual expansion so that by the mid-1970s it was serving over 20 communities in northern Argentina, from the Brazilian border down to Rosario. In 1978 it acquired two FH227s from Brazil, and the Twin Otters were sold to the Argentine Air Force. By 1984 it had changed name to ALFA (Aerolineas Federales) and it soon added Asuncion to its network. It briefly used LAERs Saab 340 on its network in 1987, but continuing financial problems forced the airline to close down by the late 1980s.

One of its two FH227s caught late one afternoon at its base of Resistencia in 1988.

AUSTRAL

The current Austral is the result of the merger between the original Austral and ALA in 1971.

Austral was set up in 1957 to fly, as its name indicates, in southern Argentina, from Buenos Aires. Its first commercial flight was in January the following year to Comodoro Rivadavia. It quickly built up a large fleet of C-46s. When Transcontinental ceased operations in 1961 Austral acquired its domestic network and fleet of C-46s. In the same year the first two DC-6s where introduced, and by 1966 Austral operated eleven of these aircraft. By this time Austral had started cooperating with ALA, leading to a full merger in 1971.

ALA was set up in Rosario in 1956 with Aerocommander 680s, but two years later acquired four DC-3s. Another two joined in 1959. When it started cooperating with Austral some DC-6s and C-46s where painted in the ALA livery.

In 1968-69 Austral & ALA took delivery of four new BAC-111-420s and three new BAC-111-520s. At the same time three new YS-11s where acquired from Japan. The BAC-111 continues to this day in the Austral fleet, although most have now been retired.

Austral has had a number of colourful liveries over the years. Initially it consisted of a simple red and black cheatline going up on the fin in a similar style to Eastern. ALA employed the same style but used a light blue and dark blue cheatline. During 1973-74 all BAC-111s where repainted all white with a six-tone band along the fuselage. This design was developed in three basic colours, green, lilac and orange. In 1976-77 it was changed again to a three colour band separated by thin white lines.

Base colours used where blue, green, brown and red/orange.

The current scheme of a red and a blue cheatline was introduced around 1978.

Today Austral's fleet consists of one BAC-111-500s, four MD-80s and eight DC-9-30s leased from Iberia.

BAC-111 LV-JNS climbs away from Aeroparque in December 1976. It carries the second version of the "colourful" livery, in this case in various shades of green. Twenty-three years after it was originally delivered LV-JNS was taken out of service in January 1993 and stored.

F-27 LV-AZV is starting its take-off roll at Aeroparque in November 1988. Its livery still carry traces of the previous owner

CATA

CATA was for many years an air-taxi operator and maintenance centre at Moron airport. However in 1987 it decided to launch a low-cost domestic air service and for this acquired two ex-Horizon Fairchild F-27s via DHC. These two where refurbished and put into service from Buenos Aires to Bariloche and Iguazu amongst other destinations.

Three more have been added. CATA also flies a CAI Arava and various R-690s.

The company is managed and owned by the Pugliese family.

LADE

Lineas Aereas del Estado (LADE) was an airline run by the Argentine Air Force to serve communities which cannot support a commercial air service. Its main operating area has always been the southern part of Argentina, from Buenos Aires all the way to Ushuaia. Before the conflict with England it also served Port Stanley.

LADE was set up in 1940 and was originally two divisions, LASO (operating in the south) and LANE (operating in the north). In 1945 the two divisions where merged as LADE. Initial equipment was mainly Junkers Ju-52s, but two ex-Air France Dewoitine D-338s where also used. During the postwar era, the DC-3s and Vickers Vikings became the main equipment although Bristol 170s where

also employed. LADE never had its own equipment but simply used aircraft from the Air Force. However in its early days many aircraft did carry the "LADE" titles, a practice that has long since been abandoned.

In 1966 LADE took over some routes from Aerolineas along with its remaining DC-3s, but they where replaced in 1969 by new Twin Otters and F-27s.

When LADE started its service to Port Stanley on the Falklands in 1972 it employed HU-16 Albatross until the

runway was completed in order to receive the F-27. The newest addition to its "fleet" was the F-28 which arrived in 1975.

LADE has lately cut back its network severely due to the financial cutbacks the Argentine Air Force is suffering. Operations were recently completely suspended.

Fokker F-28 "TC-55" taking off from Aeroparque in September 1989. The aircraft employed by LADE has always carried a basic grey/metallic colour with white top, and military serial-numbers.

LAER

Linea Aerea Entre Rios was originally set up as "LAPER" by the local province in Parana in the late 1960s to operate a scheduled regional air service using aircraft of the provincial government. First equipment was Cessna 337s, later replaced by Cessna 402s. In 1973 two new IA-50 Guarani where acquired and put into service. However in 1979 the company was disbanded. It was relaunched in 1986 as "LAER" and the IA-50s where put on the Parana-Buenos Aires and Concordia-Gualeguaychu-Buenos Aires routes. The following year a single Saab 340A was acquired from Saab, but with mounting financial problems the local government withdrew its subsidy and LAER was forced to return its flagship. Instead LAER went back to its two IA-50s until it leased three used Jetstream 31s from Bae in 1992.

With the introduction of the Saab 340 LAER launched a new livery. The 340 is seen flying over Parana in March 1988. The J-31s have a revised livery.

LAPA

Lineas Aereas Privadas Argentinas, as its full name reads, was founded in December 1977. Three new Metro IIs were purchased and put on regional routes within the Buenos Aires province. The Metros were replaced by three YS-11s purchased from Austral in 1979.

In 1980 LAPA made the headlines when it announced its intention to buy Bae-146s for new routes within Argentina. However LAPA was unable to obtain the necessary route rights. Instead it purchased two new SD-330s and concentrated on its regional network.

In September 1984 LAPA changed ownership and Andrew Deutsch became the new owner. He ordered two new Saab 340s to replace the SD-330s and briefly leased an E-110 for some small routes.

Today LAPA continues to serve communities within the province as well as its twice daily service to Colonia in Uruguay with the two 340s.

However in 1992 LAPA decided to incorporate larger aircraft, three B737s were leased for new routes in Argentina, while a B757 was wet-leased for international charters during summer the summer season.

LAPAs' two Saab 340s as seen at Aeroparque in this photo taken in March 1988.

LAS

Lineas Aereas Santafecinas was set up in the late 1980s by the province of the same name. Initial equipment was a couple of Rockwell R690s from the provincial government. LAS later leased two CASA 212s for its network within the province from its base in Rosario. However due to financial problems the C-212s were soon returned to CASA. LAS also had to scale down its operations substantially and currently serves destinations fairly sporadically.

LAS' first CASA 212 in Rosario in 1988.

SERVICIO AEREOS RIO NEGRO

This small airline was set up around 1968 in Bariloche with a single DC-3. However by the early 1970s it had ceased trading and its DC-3 was rotting away at San Justo airfield outside Buenos Aires.

Servicio Aereos Rio Negro's single DC-3 sitting in the grass at San Justo airfield, July 1977.

10

TAN

Transportes Aereos Neuquen is another local airline run by a province, in this case the Neuquen province in the south-western part of Argentina. TAN was set up in 1972 with four Piper Navajos to serve local communities around Neuquen. The Navajos were replaced by three Rockwell 690s in 1977 followed by two Metro IIIs purchased new in 1980.

Traffic continued to increase so TAN decided to move up a step by introducing a 30-seater. It purchased a single Saab 340A in 1987 to supplement the Metros on the scheduled routes. The two R690s (one had been lost in an accident) where mainly used as VIP aircraft or ambulance charters. TAN's current network has expanded in the past few years after LADE started withdrawing services. Consequently it now stretches from Cordoba in the north down via Mendoza and to Bariloche and Esquel in the south, as well as Comodoro Rivadavia and Bahia Blanca on the coast. TAN also flies across the Andes to Chile, Puerto Montt. To handle the increased services, TAN bought a third used Metro III in the USA during 1992.

STAF

STAF, or Servicios de Transportes Aereos Fueguinos SA, as its full name reads, was set up in 1985 to fly cargo to southern Argentina. A single L-188 Electra was acquired in November 1986, and it soon began making regular appearances in Miami and other places outside Argentina. In October 1990 STAF leased its L-188 to Air Bridge Carriers in England.

TAN's single Saab 340A at its home base of Neuquen in March 1988.

CL-44 LV-JZM in Miami in 1977. It has recently been broken up at Ezeiza after many years storage.
(E. Gual/Aviation Photography of Miami)

TAR

Transporte Aereo Rioplatense, as its full name reads, was formally set up in December 1969, but did not receive its first aircraft, a CL-44 until 1971. Operations began in March that year carrying cattle between Houston and Buenos Aires. TAR soon established *ad hoc* cargo charters worldwide, and thus expanded its fleet with another three similar aircraft in 1972. However, one was quickly lost in an accident in July the same year. Another was sold to AER in 1976, the same year the company initiated a fortnightly service to Basle.

Two years later TAR acquired its first jet equipment, a B-707 from Dan-Air, followed by another a year later. By this time the CL-44s/CC-106s (TAR had both variants) were gradually withdrawn from service although one crashed in July 1981 under mysterious circumstances, apparently carrying arms to Iran. The two 707s continued to be fairly active well into the 1980s, but by the mid-1980s TAR had ceased to operate, one B-707 had been withdrawn from service at Ezeiza together with the remaining CL-44 and the other B-707 parked in Miami.

TRAFE

TRAFE was set up in the early 1970s with a single CV-240 to fly charters and possibly a scheduled passenger service. However its single CV-240 soon migrated across the river to ARCO in Uruguay. TRAFE thus went into limbo until 1976 when it acquired a single ex-Delta DC-8-33 on a lease-purchase from Charlotte Aircraft. It apparently flew very few charters until TRAFE defaulted on its payments and the aircraft was impounded at Ezeiza airport, never to fly again. After more than ten years storage it was recently broken up

TRAFE's unlucky DC-8 being stored at Ezeiza airport, as seen on this photo taken in February 1987.

BOLIVIA

AEROMINAS

This is an old cargo operator based in Cochabamba, and founded in 1964 as Aerovias Las Minas. Its main equipment has been the C-46, at least fourteen having passed through its hands. It has also briefly operated DC-6 aircraft.

One of Aerominas' C-46s just after arrival at Cochabamba, November 1984. The customers are queuing up by the tailplane!

CAT

Carga Aereo Transportada, as its name implies, is another cargo outfit in La Paz. It has relied on Convair during the 1980s, at least four CV340/440s having passed through its hands.

One of CAT's CV-440s at La Paz, March 1986.

ELDORADO

Another small cargo-hauler in La Paz operating a single C-46 since 1980.

Eldorado's only aircraft, a C-46, photographed in La Paz, August 1990.

ETA

Empresa Transportes Aereos is another La Paz-based cargo airline, founded in 1977. During the 1980s it flew a single C-46 and a single DC-6. However its C-46 was lost in an accident in January 1988 when it hit mountains near La Paz, leaving the single DC-6 in operation until it was sold to CAN in 1988.

ETAs' single DC-6 at La Paz, May 1985. ETA uses the pink panther as a symbol. The DC-6 still shows the old American Airlines cheatline along the fuselage. It was originally delivered to American in 1947 and remained with them until 1966.

FRIGORIFICO SANTA RITA

This is one of the larger meat-haulers based in La Paz. It has been operating from the early 1970s until the present day, using DC-3s, C-46s and a single DC-6. However 1992 was not a good year, as it first lost a DC-3 in a ground fire in February, followed by a C-46 in March when it crashed after engine failure on take off from a ranch in Beni. The DC-3, CP-529, was one of the oldest surviving DC-3s in Bolivia, having been delivered to LAB in 1945 and thus survived over forty-six years of flying in Bolivia.

This was the unlucky C-46 which was lost in March 1992. It is pictured at La Paz in May 1985 on a rather crowded ramp area!

FRI-REYES

Fri-Reyes, or "Frigorifico Reyes", as its full name goes, is the largest of the so-called "meat-haulers" in La Paz. It has been flying since the 1960s, and became famous for being the last airline to use Boeing B-17s well into the 1970s. The last two were sold in the US for restoration. Instead Fri-Reyes purchased eight CV-240s from surplus USAF stocks in the 1970s. Four DC-4s were also bought in the US during the late 1970s, plus a fifth ex-Argentine DC-4 in 1980 which had been stored for many years in Asuncion.

In 1981 Fri-Reyes acquired all surviving piston aircraft from Faucett in Peru, namely two DC-4s and two DC-6s. Another DC-6 came from the Chilean Air Force in 1982. A Martin 404 was briefly used in the mid-1980s, so was an ex-Mexican CV-440.

By the early 1990s its fleet had been reduced to just a few aircraft, both by accidents and dwindling business.

One of Fri-Reyes DC-6s, caught in La Paz in May 1985. This particular aircraft came from the Chilean Air Force in 1982. Notice the CV-240 and the nose of the last B-17 in the background!

LAB

The national airline of Bolivia is the second oldest airline in Latin America, which survives to the present day (The first was SCADTA/Avianca in Colombia). LAB was founded by local Germans in 1925 with a single Junkers F-13. The German influence can be noticed in the name, "Lloyd Aereo Boliviano". In December 1925 it flew the first service from Cochabamba to Santa Cruz. The following year LAB began flying to Trinidad in the north, followed by Puerto Suarez, Yacuiba, La Paz and Riberalta in 1928. LAB now had six F-13s, and added its first Junkers W-34 in 1929. In 1932 Junkers Ju-52s and a single Ford Trimotor arrived. After a Junkers 86 arrived in 1937, LAB connected its network with Sindicato Condor in Brazil, and Lufthansa-Peru thus offering a trans-continental air service.

In May 1941 LAB was nationalized, and subsequently Panagra acquired 23 per cent of the airline. L. Lodestars were introduced to replace the Junkers. During the postwar period, LAB acquired DC-3s and Boeing 17s, the latter being considered suitable for both cargo and passenger service. LAB operated no less than eleven during the 1950s and early 1960s. LAB also bought eight C-46s, which quickly became popular in Bolivia, several being still in use.

In 1954 LAB began a cautious foreign expansion by adding Arica in Chile to the network. The following year two DC-4s arrived. Corumba followed in 1957, Porto Velho and Asuncion in 1958, and finally Buenos Aires in 1959. A third DC-4 and the first of four DC-6Bs followed in 1960. The early 1960s put a financial strain on the airline, and various foreign consultants were used. First turboprop equipment

arrived in 1968 in the shape of a single L.Electra followed by two new Fairchild F-27s in 1969. The big step came in 1970, when LAB placed its first B-727-100 in service on March 14, between Cochabamba and La Paz. Another five B727s followed during the 1970s, and they form the backbone of the present LAB fleet. In the 1980s two B-707s were employed.

LAB entered the widebody era in November 1989 when it leased a B-767 from Britannia. It was mainly employed on the Miami route, but was returned in January 1990. Instead LAB opted for the A-310. The first was leased from Royal Jordanian in June 1991, but returned two months later. It was replaced by another leased from ILFC in November 1991. Like Pluna and LAP, the Bolivian government has announced its intention to privatize LAB.

LAB's first B-727, CP-861, pictured at Santa Cruz "Viru Viru" airport in July 1984. LAB's livery has remained fairly unchanged since this B-727 arrived in 1970.

LAB's two original F-27s were lost in accidents, so another four second-hand ones were bought between 1974 and 1977. However, no less than three were lost in accidents between 1980 and 1984. To fill the shortage, LAB leased two from TAT from January 1985 to August 1987. These were flown in basic TAT livery as shown by F-GBRV at Cochabamba in February 1985. These two were replaced by two used Fokker F-27s.

La Cumbre's stored DC-6, seen at La Paz, May 1985. It still carries the basic VASP cheatline.

LA CUMBRE

This La Paz-based cargo company was founded in 1974 with two C-46s. In 1977 it purchased two DC-6s from VASP plus a third in the USA, this was however soon lost in an accident. The C-46s have been withdrawn, and one DC-6 cannibalized, leaving a single DC-6 in service.

LINEAS AEREAS CANEDO

This Cochabamba-based airline began operations around 1981 flying both cargo and passengers with four DC-3s. It has since sold all DC-3s, and now flies light aircraft.

One of Canedo's DC-3s at Cochabamba, November 1984. Displaying its "pre-war" passenger door, this DC-3 was originally delivered to PennCentral in 1939. It came to Bolivia in 1975.

NEBAs' current aircraft is this single C-46, photographed in Cochabamba, May 1985.

NEBA

NEBA, North East Bolivian Airways, is a small cargo airline based in Cochabamba. It has mainly relied on a single CV-440 and a single C-46 during the 1980s. However, its CV-440 was lost in an emergency landing on 11th May, 1990 near Cochabamba, leaving the airline with the C-46.

PANAMBRA

This small cargo airline based in La Paz began operations around 1980 with a single CV-440. After it was lost in an accident another was purchased from Fri-Reyes.

Panambra's single CV-440, purchased from Fri-Reyes. It is pictured at La Paz in March 1986.

SAB

Servicios Aereos Bolivianos is another long-time cargo operator. It began operations in 1970 and flew C-46s throughout the 1970s and early 1980s. It also employed a couple of B-25s.

One of SABs' C-46s at Cochabamba, November 1984.

SAVCO

SAVCO was founded in 1970, and its name derives from "Servicios Aereos Virgen de Copacabana". It has employed mostly C-46s and DC-3s, but also briefly flew two DC-6s in the early 1970s. Its fleet had dwindled to a single DC-3 by the late 1980s

SAVCO's surviving DC-3, caught at Cochabamba, November 1984. This DC-3 was originally flown by the Spanish Air Force, and came to Bolivia via Aces High in England in 1981.

One of TAB's C-130s caught in Miami, one of its regular destinations, in 1977.
(Author's collection)

TAB

TAB is a cargo airline operated by the Bolivian Air Force. It was set up in 1977 with C-130s, of which it soon built up a fleet of four. One was however shot down in Angola, when it was leased to another operator. TAB has lately added a single DC-8.

TASS

TASS, or Transporte Aereos Samuel Selum, as its full name reads, was founded in 1984 in la Paz. It has used Martin 404 aircraft, but its single M404 was lost in an accident after take off from La Paz on April 7th, 1990.

TASS Martin 404 taxying in La Paz, July 1984.

TRANSALFA

This was one of the few cargo haulers based in Santa Cruz. It was founded in 1981 with DC-3s, and later operated a single CV-440 before going out of business in the late 1980s.

Transalfa's single CV-440 shortly after its delivery from the USA, photographed in Santa Cruz, October 1984. It was later registered CP-1961.

TRANSPORTES AEREOS AMERICA

This small cargo airline is based in La Paz and flew a single CV-440 during the 1980s.

Its single CV-440 caught at La Paz, March 1986.

TRANS AEREOS LUWIOR

This small cargo airline was founded in 1979 in Cochabamba. It operated C-46s during the 1980s.

One of its C-46s shares the ramp at Cochabamba with LAB's 727s. It features a rather simple livery!

TRANS AEREOS SAN MIGUEL

This Cochabamba-based cargo company was founded in 1981 with DC-3, of which it has used at least four.

One of its rather attractive DC-3s at Cochabamba, November 1984.

UNIVERSAL

This freight company began operations around 1977, with two C-46s, both remaining in service until January 1990, when one was lost in an emergency landing after engine failure during take off from La Paz.

Universal's surviving C-46 still carries the basic TABA livery from whom it was purchased in 1981. Before TABA it flew for Transair in Sweden and the Congo.

YACUMA

This small cargo company is based in La Paz and was founded in 1981. It flies a single CV-340 (C-131) bought from surplus USAF stocks.

Yacuma's CV-340 firing up at La Paz in May, 1985.

BRAZIL

CRUZEIRO DO SUL

Cruzeiro began as "Syndicato Condor", which began operations between Rio de Janeiro and Porto Alegre in 1927. The airline was set up with substantial backing from German interests, and its first aircraft were Dornier Walls and Junkers G-24. In 1930 it extended its network along the coast to Natal. Syndicato Condor also established a mail service by linking up with fast surface ships to Europe. During the 1930s Syndicato Condor introduced Junkers F-13s, Ju-52s, W-33/34s, Ju-46s and finally a pair of FW-200 Condor in 1939. However the rapid change of events in Europe forced a change of status for Syndicato Condor. In 1941 its name was changed to "Servicios Aereos Condor", and its German management was gradually exchanged for Brazilian. At this time Syndicato Condor was operating sixteen Ju-52s, two Fw-200s, two Fw-58s, six Junkers W-34s and two Junkers F-13s. Another name change followed in 1943 when the airline became known as "Servicios Aereos Cruzeiro do Sul". At the same time it started introducing American equipment, first DC-3s in 1943 followed by Lockheed 12 in 1945 and Beech AT-11 and DC-4s in 1946.

In 1947 Cruzeiro was given the authorization to start flying to the USA, but since it would not receive subsidies it refused to start services. The DC-4s intended for this were sold, instead Cruzeiro began flying to Georgetown in British Guyana, and to Santa Cruz in Bolivia. In 1954 Cruzeiro purchase CV-340s and thus became the first Brazilian airline to introduce pressurized equipment. By 1955 it had eighteen of these twins. In 1958 it introduced Fairchild C-82s for cargo and carrying engines.

Its first order for jet aircraft came in 1961 when it ordered four Caravelles which entered service in 1963. When Panair do Brazil collapsed in 1965 Cruzeiro took over its domestic network (and Varig the international). With it Cruzeiro inherited three Caravelles and five PBY Catalinas for services in the Amazon. The following year Cruzeiro ordered eight new YS-11s to replace the Convairs. Two years later it continued its re-equipment programme by ordering four B-727-100s and these entered service in 1970. They were later followed by B-737s.

On 22nd May, 1975 Cruzeiro was taken over by Varig, but allowed to continue as a separate company under its old identity. At this time Cruzeiro had a fleet of one DC-3, five YS-11s, five Caravelles, eight B727-100s, and six B737s.

In 1979 Cruzeiro ordered two A-300s plus two options, which were converted in 1980. The first two A-300s arrived in 1980, but the other two were taken over by Varig. By this time its fleet had been rationalized to consist of six B737s, eight B-727s and two A-300s. This fleet would stay fairly unchanged during the 1980s.

In 1992 Varig announced that Cruzeiro would be absorbed by Varig, thus the name Cruzeiro would disappear.

This B-727 photographed at Buenos Aires-Ezeiza airport in December 1974 shows the livery used by Cruzeiro during the late 1960s and early 1970s.

In the mid-1970s Cruzeiro introduced a new livery, as shown on this B-737 at Sao Paulo-Congonhas airport in June 1976.

NORDESTE

This regional airline based in the north-eastern part of Brazil began operations in June 1976 with Bandeirantes. It took over routes and Bandeirantes from Transbrasil, with Transbrasil acquiring 33 per cent of the new regional airline based in Salvador. It built up a fleet of six Bandits by 1980, painted in a striking yellow livery. By 1985 it had eight Bandits, but still no larger aircraft due to the fairly thin routes it flew. Instead its Bandit fleet continued to grow, thirteen were in service by 1990.

In 1992 it announced an order for three Fokker 50s, but it was unable to take delivery of these new 50-seaters (they were resold to Rio-Sul), instead it acquired a few Brasilias

An early shot of a Nordeste Bandeirante, taken in Belo Horizonte, June 1976. It later changed livery to a basic blue colour scheme.

This F-27 at Santos Dumont airport in Rio de Janeiro (notice the Sugarloaf in the background!) it shows the Rio Sul livery in blue/white. (Author's collection)

RIO-SUL

This regional airline based in Rio de Janeiro, was founded in 1976 out of a local air-taxi company and with the assistance of Varig, who acquired 52 per cent of the shares. Initial equipment was again the Brazilian-produced Bandeirante and PA-31 Navajos, and operations began in August 1976 within the Rio Grande state. By 1980 it had a fleet of eight Emb-110s, two PA-31s and a single Sabreliner. In 1982 it moved up to 50-seaters by acquiring three Fokker F-27-200s. It later added another four. However they were soon replaced by Emb-120 Brasilias which started arriving in the late 1980s, nine being in service by 1990. In 1992 Rio-Sul took over Nordestes order for three F-50s, closely followed by the first B737-500.

TABA

TABA, or Transportes Aereos de Bacia Amazonic, began operations in July 1975 in the Amazon region. The airline started as a result of the subsidies initiated by the Brazilian government in 1975 to support a regional air service. The first routes were from Belem to Itaituba and Manaus. Initial equipment was Beech 18, but it quickly acquired Emb-110 Bandeirantes and C-46s. By 1980 its fleet had grown to five Beech 18s, ten Emb-110s, one C-46 and two FH-227s. The FH-227s were leased in 1976, and later bought. TABA was also an early operator of the Bae 146-100, taking delivery of two in December 1983. However it did not become successful in the TABA operation, and both were returned to Bae in 1985. Instead TABA acquired more FH-227s, having six by 1985. The last C-46 was sold in Bolivia (see Universal of Bolivia). By 1990 a seventh FH-227 had arrived, but TABA then decided to start replacing the FH-227s with DHC-8-300s leased from GPA, four having arrived by 1992. Latest passenger statistics, for 1991, show 205,000 passengers carried. The airline is owned and managed by the Gibson family. The most recent development has been the inauguration of its first international route in 1992, to Georgetown via Boa Vista.

A line-up of TABA "Bandits" in Manaus, February 1987. TABA initially used a white-brown-blue livery as shown on Universal's C-46, but this was changed to the current blue-white in the early 1980s.

TAM

This regional airline based in Sao Paulo grew out of an air-taxi company that was established in 1961. VASP acquired 38 per cent of this regional airline when it began operations in July 1976. VASP also handed over the Emb-110s that it had been operating under its own name. Thus TAM started off with nine Emb-110s and six Cessna 402s. TAM also moved up to 50-seaters fairly quickly, by 1985 it had six Fokker F-27s in service, another two arrived by 1988.

The next big step came in September 1990, when TAM leased two Fokker 100s. By 1993 TAM operated eight F-100s along with nine F27s and three Bandeirantes.

One of TAM's Emb-110s caught in Campo Grande, February 1987.

This 1972 photograph shows an HP Herald still portraying the old Sadia name and livery. (Author's collection)

By the mid-1970s it had changed its name to Transbrasil and introduced this very colourful livery, as seen on this BAC-111 in Brasilia, June 1976.

TRANSBRASIL

Transbrasil was set up as Sadia in 1955 by Omar Fontana, initially to improve the distribution of meat from his father's meat-packing plant. Operations began in 1956 with a DC-3 from Sao Paulo to Florianopolis via Joacaba and Videira. In 1957 Sadia formed an alliance with REAL. The network was expanded to Rio de Janeiro and Porto Alegre, and C-46s were introduced.

After REAL's collapse in 1961 Sadia took over TAS, a small airline in Salvador. Its fleet was by now twelve DC-3s and three C-46s.

In January 1965 Sadia ordered five Heralds to replace the DC-3s. The Herald was soon followed by the BAC-111. Sadia ordered this type in February 1969 and it entered service the following year.

After Sadia changed its name to Transbrasil it ordered six EMB-110 Bandeirantes in 1973 for its smaller routes. At the same time it introduced a new colourful livery, painting each aircraft in different colours. By the mid-1970s, Transbrasil had a fleet of six EMB-110s, three HP Heralds, seven BAC-111s and two newly arrived B727s. The Heralds were on the way out, and the Bandeirantes were soon to be handed over to Noroeste. The BAC-111s survived until the late 1970s, when Transbrasil went all B-727, having fifteen by 1980. Instead it ordered nine B757s and three B767s. However its financial situation soon forced it to cancel the 757 order and just take delivery of the 767s. During the mid-1980s it acquired a fleet of second-hand B707s for both passenger and cargo services. The late 1980s saw the withdrawal of the 707s and 727s, so by 1990 Transbrasil operated the three B767s, three B707s and fifteen B737-300/400s, the latter all leased from different sources. Transbrasil had by now expanded to the international arena, adding services to Washington, Miami and Orlando in the USA. Later New York was added. Current plans call for new services to Europe, including Russia.

VARIG

Varig is another old-timer in the South American skies, it is the fourth oldest surviving airline in Latin America. It flew its first service on 22nd June, 1927. For the first fifteen years it confined its operations around Porto Alegre, hence its name was derived from "Viacao Aerea Rio Grandense", Rio Grande being the name of the local state. Varig had close cooperation with German aviation interests at this time, hence its initial equipment, a single Dornier Wal and a Merkur came from Germany. As mentioned earlier, Varig confined its initial developments to within the state until 1942. Varig struggled with various small aircraft, and had to be reorganized in 1932 with the state lending money in order to acquire two Junkers F-13s and two Junkers A-50s. A Messerschmitt M20b arrived in 1937, followed by a single Ju-52 the following year. Varig opened its first route outside the state in 1942 when it began flying to Montevideo in Uruguay. In the same year it acquired two non-German aircraft when it purchased a single Fiat G.2 and DH.89A Dragon Rapide. The first American equipment arrived in 1943 in the shape of Lockheed L.10 Electras, followed by the first of many DC-3s in 1946. Varig also operated twenty Curtiss C-46s during the 1950s.

In 1953 Varig was nominated as one of two airlines to serve North America. For this purpose it ordered three new L.1049G Constellations. With this equipment the Rio de Janeiro to New York route was inaugurated in August 1955. The route was soon extended in the other direction to Buenos Aires.

Otherwise the 1950s were fairly uneventful, except for the introduction of Convair 240s in 1957. In the same year it also ordered two Caravelles and three B-707s. The Caravelle entered service in 1959. In the same year Varig got involved in the Rio de Janeiro-Sao Paulo airbridge together with VASP and Cruzeiro do Sul. Varig employed its CV-240s on this service.

The big leap forward came in August 1961 when Varig took over REAL, another large Brazilian airline. At this time REAL had a large fleet of DC-3s, C-46s, CV-340/440s and L-1049 Constellations. It had ordered new CV-990s which were delivered directly to Varig. It also inherited REAL's extensive international network. In the same year Varig ordered five L.188 Electras, and thus began an association with this aircraft that was going to last for thirty years. It soon proved to be the ideal aircraft for the airbridge.

The next big leap forward came in February 1965 when Varig took over Panair do Brazil and its international network. Through this take-over Varig acquired more Caravelles and DC-8s. Varig had now established itself as the major Brazilian airline on the world market. After the take-over of Panair, Varig now flew to New York, Miami and Los Angeles in the USA, seven destinations in Europe,

and Caracas, Lima, Bogota, Asuncion, Santiago and Buenos Aires in South America plus Mexico City in Central America. Varig also began flying to Johannesburg in 1970.

The late 1960s also saw the introduction of the HS.748s to replace the remaining DC-3s. However, the last 748s were sold in 1976.

Fleetwise, the DC-8 and CV-990s were phased out, instead Varig built up a fleet of sixteen B-707s by the mid-1970s, by which time it had introduced its first DC-10-30. Varig ordered ten new B-737s in 1974, after having introduced the B-727-100 in 1970. These two aircraft types were to become the backbone of the domestic and neighbouring countries routes.

The DC-10s did not become the only widebodies in the Varig fleet. In 1981 Varig added three new B747s and two new A-300s. More 747s of the new -300 version followed in 1985, and new B-767s were added from 1986.

By 1990 its fleet consisted of fourteen Electras, twenty-one B-737s (including leased -300s), ten B727-100s, ten B-767s, twelve DC-10-30s and eight B-747s. The Electras were finally retired in 1992 from the airbridge between Rio de Janeiro and Sao Paulo, replaced by B737s. Meanwhile Varig received its first two MD-11s and B747-400s. In January 1993 Cruzeiro will be completely absorbed into Varig.

One of its DC-10s on approach to Madrid, January 1990. Varig's livery has remained fairly unchanged since the 1950s, with its blue cheatline and titles.

This cargo DC-6 stored at Sao Paulo-Congonhas, shows the VASP livery of the 1960s. PP-LFA was photographed in May 1976. It was sold to La Cumbre as CP-1283 in Bolivia in 1977, see La Cumbre entry.

many leased aircraft. Its fleet during 1990 consisted of twenty-one B-737-200s, eight leased B-737-300s and three A-300s. The B727s had been sold.

Later, DC-10-30s were leased for the US charter flights and DC-8-70s for cargo operations. However, VASP entered severe economic problems in late 1992, and many of the leased aircraft were repossessed.

One of VASP's B-737s showing the livery used during the 1970s. PP-SMY was photographed in Brasilia, May 1976.

VASP

Viacao Aerea Sao Paulo SA, was founded, as its name implies, in Sao Paulo in 1933 by local state, City and Municipal bank. Operations began in April 1934 with two Monospar ST.4s imported from England. A single DH.84 followed later in the same year. VASP began flying two routes, to Sao Paulo-Ribeirao Preto-Uberaba and Sao Paulo-Sao Carlos-Rio Preto. In 1936 VASP acquired two Ju-52s from Germany and began flying to Rio de Janeiro. The Ju-52s kept flying during the war, however spares were becoming increasingly difficult to acquire. Once the war ended VASP quickly built up a fleet of sixteen DC-3s to replace the German aircraft. At the same time the network was gradually extended. In February 1949 VASP assumed the control of Aerovias Brazil, and via Aerovias VASP acquired Saab Scandias. Happy with these aircraft, VASP later ordered more Scandias directly from Sweden.

In May 1957 VASP took a big step up by ordering five Viscount 827s. In July 1959 VASP signed a pool agreement with Varig and Cruzeiro to jointly operate the Sao Paulo-Rio de Janeiro air bridge. VASP supplied Scandias for the air bridge.

In January 1962 VASP took over Loide. After this take-over VASP served 72 cities within Brazil.

The next big step came in 1967 when VASP ordered two new BAC-111s, followed by an order for six YS-11s the following year. However VASP soon switched to the B-737, and received the first of these twin-jets in 1969. For the local network VASP introduced Bandeirantes in 1973. VASP continued upgrading its fleet, ordering B-727-200s in 1977. By this time its propeller fleet was dwindling, with YS-11s and DC-6s on the way out. Instead the B-737 became the backbone of the fleet. In 1980 its fleet

consisted of twenty-one B-737s and twelve B-727s. The Bandeirantes were turned over to TAM, in which VASP had a minority shareholding. To handle its bigger routes, VASP ordered three A-300s in January 1981, and nine A-310s the following year. However the A-310s were cancelled the year after when VASP entered financial problems.

In the mid-1980s VASP began flying charters to Florida, Netherlands, Antilles and Argentina. In 1989 it began its first scheduled international route, to Aruba. In 1990 VASP was privatized, and immediately launched an aggressive expansion. It added ten domestic destinations and to handle this it used

VOTEC

This was the fifth regional airline formed in 1976 as a consequence of the subsidies being introduced for regional air service. It also grew out of an air-taxi company founded in 1966. Votec continued to operate as a different division, one being air-taxi, another the regional air service with BN2A Islanders and Bandeirantes. By 1980 its regional business employed eleven Bandeirantes, five DC-3s and thirteen BN2A Islanders. It also soon moved up to F-27s, employing three by 1985. Shortly afterwards the regional airline was completely reorganized under a new name, "Brazil Central" with a new livery. Its fleet remained fairly stable, by 1990 it employing eight Bandeirantes and two F-27s.

One of its F-27s showing the new Brazil Central livery. (Author's collection)

Aerocor's two DC-3s at Los Cerillos airport, November 1986.

CHILE

AEROCOR

Aerolineas Cordillera, as its full name reads, was a small airline flying two DC-3s and a number of light aircraft including a GAF Nomad during the late 1970s and 1980s. It has since ceased operations.

AERONOR

This small Santiago-based airline was founded in 1977, and began operations with F-27s three years later. It was closely associated with a newspaper and mainly carried newspapers, although some scheduled passenger service was flown as well. From 1978 to 1981 it purchased six Fairchild F-27s on the second-hand market. Two were lost in accidents in 1979 and 1982, while a third was sold to a small scheduled passenger airline called TAC. Aeronor kept operating its remaining three F-27s plus a Metro until 1986 when it ceased operations and its aircraft were stored.

One of its F-27s at Los Cerillos shortly after it ceased operations, November 1986.

One of Aspar's Catalinas at Los Cerillos, November 1986.

ASPAR

Aeroservicios Parrague, or simply Aspar, was founded in 1959 when it acquired its first PBY Catalina aircraft, followed by a second in 1960. Aspar then settled in on air-taxi work including regular flights to Easter Island and Tahiti. In 1970 it converted its first Catalina as a water-bomber, and this soon became its main business. Later a second Catalina was converted. Its operations soon expanded to Argentina, and in the last few years they have operated in Spain.

FAST AIR

Fast Air began all-cargo operations late in 1978 after it purchased a single B-707 from TWA. A second B-707 was added in 1988. Fast Air mainly flies between Chile and the US (Miami). In November 1992 it leased two DC-8-71Fs from GPA to replace its 707s. In 1994 it was taken over by LAN-Chile.

One of Fast Air's B-707s taking off from Miami, November 1991.

LADECO

Ladeco was formed in November 1958 to take over the domestic network left by the bankruptcy of Cinta-Ala. Cinta had started a scheduled passenger service in 1951 between Chile and Miami. Ladeco was closely associated with the copper mines, hence its initials stood for "Linea Aerea del Cobre". It began a domestic scheduled passenger service with DC-3s. It acquired two DC-6Bs from American in 1966, later followed by another four. In the early 1970s Ladeco served Calama, Antofagasta, El Salvador (mine), Puerto Montt and Balmaceda from its base in Santiago, with DC-6s. In 1976 it purchased its first B727-100 from Braniff followed by two more in 1978-79. This enabled the last DC-6 to be retired and sold in the US. In 1979 Ladeco entered the international arena by beginning services to Asuncion, Mendoza, Rio de Janeiro and Sao Paulo. In the 1980s, Ladeco continued with its three B727s plus two B737-200s which arrived in 1980. The 737s were then sold and Ladeco just flew 727s in the second half of the 1980s. It then expanded rapidly, leasing two F27s for domestic services, and a couple of B707s for cargo and passenger services. It soon went back to B737s and also leased two BAC-111s, again for domestic services. By 1994 the fleet consisted of two leased B757s, two B707s, four B727s, eight B737s and four BAC-111s.

The DC-6s featured a simple blue cheatline, but when the B727 arrived Ladeco launched this orange-yellow livery. This B727 was photographed at Rio-Galleao airport, November 1987.

Ladeco now uses this original livery, as seen on one of its B707s at Mexico City, November 1992.

LAN-CHILE

This national airline of Chile was organized in 1929 as "Linea Aeropostal Santiago-Arica", and its first route was as the name suggests, Santiago-Arica flown with DH.60 Gipsy Moths with several stops on the way. In 1930 three Ford Trimotors were introduced, these having been bought by the Chilean Air Force. Two years later the airline was separated from the Air Force, and became an independent government agency, at the same time it was renamed "Linea Aerea Nacional" or simply "LAN". Potez 56s, Curtiss Condors and four-seat Fairchilds were soon added. Three Junkers 86s followed in 1938. During the early 1940s LAN acquired six Lockheed 10s and four Lockheed Lodestars.

The first international route, to Buenos Aires, was opened in 1946 with Lodestars, at the same time LAN introduced the first DC-3s. The following year four brand-new Martin 202s augmented the fleet, at the same time the Buenos Aires route was extended to Montevideo. In 1949-50 twelve DH.104 Doves were purchased in England for the domestic network. Three new DC-6Bs arrived in 1955, followed by four more in 1958. By now LAN had become known as "LAN-Chile", and the international network now included La Paz, Lima, and Mendoza. Miami was added in August 1958.

LAN-Chile became a jet operator in 1964 when three new SE210 Caravelles were delivered, but to increase its domestic fleet, three second-hand DC-6Bs were purchased from Western the following year. A DC-6 inaugurated the route to Easter Island in 1967. In the same year an ex-Lufthansa B707 was delivered and inaugurated the New York route on April 15th. At the same time, nine new HS.748s were purchased to replace the remaining

DC-3s on the domestic network. The final part of the re-equipment came in 1968 when four new B727-100s were delivered to replace the remaining DC-6s, although the final examples were not sold until 1973-74.

A second B-707 arrived late in 1969, and the following year LAN opened its first route across the Atlantic when it inaugurated a service to Frankfurt via Paris and Madrid on 1st August. Meanwhile the Pacific route had been extended to Tahiti in 1968, followed by Fiji in 1974. During the 1970s LAN acquired another six B-707s on the second-hand market. Meanwhile the three Caravelles were sold

LAN's current livery is shown on this B-767 in Miami, 1990.
(E. Gual/Aviation Photography of Miami)

to Aerotal in Colombia in 1975, followed by the phase-out of the 748s in 1978 and the B727s in 1979.

For the long-haul routes LAN-Chile began operating DC-10-30s in 1980, and two remained until 1986 when they were replaced by the B-767. B-737 arrived in 1980 for the domestic network.

LAN-Chile became one of the first South American airlines to be privatized when, in 1989, a local group, Icarosan, together with SAS bought the airline, and subsequently restructured it. Due to heavy losses its ambitious re-equipment plans were soon cut back. SAS has recently sold its shares to a group of local businessmen. The current fleet is three B707 cargoes, two Bae-146s, three B737s and four B767s.

LASA

Linea Aerea Sud Americana, as its initials stand for, began operations in the early 1960s, mostly non-scheduled cargo flights. During the 1960s it flew at least four different C-46s, and then bought two DC-6Bs from Lan-Chile in 1974. Operations continued on a small scale, and it ceased operations in the early 1980s.

One of LASA's C-46s caught in 1977.
(Author's collection)

ACES initially used an all-red livery on its ST-27s, but the arrival of the Twin Otters in the mid-1970s marked a change of the colour scheme to white with orange, as shown on this Twin Otter in Medellin, August 1986.

The ATR-42s introduced the current livery, as shown on this B727 in Miami, July 1992.

COLOMBIA

ACES

This private airline was founded as a regional carrier in August 1971 by Alvaro Arango and the Coulson family. It began operations from Medellin the following year with Saunders ST-27s. The airline grew rapidly, it flew 100,000 passengers in 1975, and 432,000 by 1980. Over a million passengers were carried two years later. The ST-27s were quickly replaced with a large fleet of DH Twin Otters, over twenty were purchased directly from DH, of which a few survive today. ACES acquired a single FH-227 in 1977 followed by a few more in the 1980s, but the big step came in 1981 when ACES began operating four B727-100s leased from Eastern. This aircraft has since become its main equipment with B727-200s being leased recently to use on the new Miami route. The FH-227s have been replaced by four ATR-42s leased from GPA. Some Twin Otters remain for local services.

This Electra caught in Miami in 1975 shows the livery used until its demise in 1981. (Author's collection)

AEROCONDOR

Aerocondor became the biggest airline in Colombia after Avianca, until it declared bankruptcy in June 1981 and its aircraft were impounded all over Colombia and in Miami. Its beginnings were modest, it began flying cargo with C-46s in 1957 after it was founded two years earlier. With new DC-4s it began passenger services in 1960, and soon upgraded to DC-6s in 1963. Aerocondor then began flying cargo to Miami, but it soon received permission to begin passenger services to this Florida gateway. The DC-4s were replaced in 1968-69 with a fleet of ex-American L188 Electras. American also became the source of supply in 1972 when Aerocondor acquired its first B720. An even bigger step came in 1977 when Aerocondor became the first South American airline to order an A300, a single aircraft arrived in December and was mainly used for the Miami service. However, Aerocondor started experiencing financial problems, first the A300 was repossessed by Airbus in 1979, and Aerocondor went back to its B707s and B720s until it finally succumbed two years later.

AEROLINEAS TAO

This small all-passenger airline began in the early 1960s with DC-3s from Neiva. It traded initially as Taxi Aereo Opita, but then changed to Aerolineas TAO. Two Viscount 700s were purchased from Alitalia in 1968, a third followed in 1969. (A fourth was bought for spares). However, soon after a bad accident in June 1974 when one of its Viscounts hit a mountain near Cucuta with the loss of 44 lives, it ceased operations in 1974. The two surviving Viscounts were stored in Bogota. An attempt was made to later relaunch the airline with a C-46.

The two Viscounts in storage in Bogota, 1975. HK-1057 became a unique Viscount by having a new wing fitted after an accident in 1971. Its livery mainly consists of the original Alitalia paint scheme.
(Author's collection)

AEROSUCRE

This is another all-cargo company operating in Bogota whose operations go back to 1969. It also flew C-46s in the beginning of its career, and moved up to DC-6s in 1976-77 followed by a single DC-4 in 1979.

Its first turbine equipment was introduced in 1981 when it purchased two HP Heralds from BAF in England, both of these were later lost in accidents. Instead Aerosucre followed the path of several previous Colombian operators by acquiring its first Caravelle in 1982 from Spain. More Caravelles followed including two recently purchased from Sterling in Denmark. Aerosucre also acquired a couple of ex-Avianca 727s in 1992. The current fleet consists of two DC -6s, three Caravelles and three B-727s.

One of its Herald's photographed in Curacao, January 1986. This airport plus Aruba are regular destinations for Aerosucre.

AEROTACA

This regional airline based in Bogota is part of a large air-taxi and general aviation group in Colombia. For the regional services it employs three Twin Otters but has just ordered one Brasilia.

One of Aerotaca's Twin Otters in Bogota, November 1992, showing the current livery. The previous featured different cartoons on the fin.

One of several B727s operated by Aerotal, this one was caught in 1981. It was hijacked the following year, during the attempt to land in Cali, it hit vehicles blocking the runway, and was badly damaged, never to fly again. (ALPS)

AEROTAL

Aerotal was set up as an air-taxi company in 1971, but soon moved up to DC-3s. DC-4s from Avianca soon followed, and Aerotal expanded its network of scheduled services from Bogota to a number of domestic points. First jet aircraft, in the shape of three ex-LAN Chile Caravelles arrived in 1975, three more arrived in 1978-79 along with a couple of leased B707s. Aerotal continued its expansion in the early 1980s with B727s and more 707s. By now its financial situation had deteriorated, hence it suspended operations in 1983 and several of its aircraft were to litter the airport for many years to come, embroiled in the aftermath of the bankruptcy.

AIRES

This scheduled regional airline based in Bogota was founded in 1981. It initially acquired five E-110 Bandeirantes and this aircraft is still used on the thin routes. For the larger routes Aires has added four Fairchild F-27s.

One of Aires' four F-27s at Bogota in November 1992. It features the new blue livery, which has replaced the original red colour scheme.

ARCA

ARCA, or Aerovias Colombianas, as its full name goes, is another old-timer in the all-cargo market. Operations began originally out of Villavicencio with DC-3s in 1960. A single C-46 was used from 1969 to 1975 when its DC-3 was sold to Aerosucre. Instead a single DC-6 was purchased, which remained for a long time.

After having leased a B707 for a short period, ARCA acquired its first two DC-8s from Alitalia in 1977. Two DC-8s continue to be its main equipment on its all-cargo flights.

This was ARCAs' first DC-8, acquired in February 1977, and it still carries the cheatline from the original operator, Alitalia. It now lies in a field outside Eldorado airport.

AVESCA

This all-cargo airline was founded in Bogota in 1983. Initial aircraft were C-46s, but by the late 1980s it had added CV-580s. A single CV-580 remains in the fleet, which now consists of three ex-Cruzeiro B727-100s purchased during 1992.

One of Avesca's B727s at Bogota, November 1992. It still features the basic Cruzeiro livery.

One of Avianca's many B727-100s caught in 1976, with the older Avianca livery. (Author's collection)

AVIANCA

This main airline of Colombia is the oldest surviving airline in Latin America. It began operations in September 1921 as SCADTA. However it was actually founded two years earlier, in December 1919, by a local group of Germans, and hence its initial equipment was the Junkers F-13. First route was from Bogota/Girardot to Barranquilla, followed by a second route to Buenaventura in 1927. With considerable technical and financial support from Germany, SCADTA was able to expand rapidly using mainly Junkers aircraft. Due to financial problems, Pan Am was able to acquire 84 per cent of SCADTA between 1930 and 1931.

On 8th June, 1940 SCADTA changed its name to Avianca, and merged at the same time with another local airline called SACO. DC-3s and Boeing 247s were introduced. The DC-3s were going to stay with Avianca until the early 1970s, at least forty-eight were used. First international routes were inaugurated in 1947 to Miami and Balboa. During the 1940s Avianca continued to use Ford Trimotors, Junkers W34 and light aircraft on its domestic network. New York followed in 1948. During the period 1947 to 1952 Avianca absorbed six domestic airlines, of which the biggest was LANSA with a fleet of DC-3s and DC-4s. DC-4s also became a

popular aircraft, being in service from 1947 to the mid-1970s. New L. Constellations arrived in 1951. The other big route expansion came in 1950 with the start of services to Europe (Lisbon, Madrid, Paris, Frankfurt and Hamburg). After passing via Super Constellations, Avianca introduced jets in 1961 with the arrival of two new B720s. At the same time Avianca began flying to Mexico City and Buenos Aires. These 720s replaced piston-engined aircraft on the international network. With the arrival of the first B727-100 and HS.748 in 1966 and 1968 respectively, Avianca could start retiring its large domestic piston fleet including the last Connies. However, the last piston-engined aircraft did not leave until the mid-1970s, after being used as cargo aircraft. At the same time the first B747 arrived, making Avianca an all-jet operator by 1976. Meanwhile Avianca had introduced an all-new red livery in the early 1970s, replacing its previous white-blue colours. With the arrival of the B747 Avianca modified its red livery and this is still in use. By 1980 Avianca had a fleet of two B747s, ten B707/720s, seven B727-200s and ten B727-100s. During the 1980s Avianca gradually retired the older B707s and B720s, and at the same time introduced B767s. By 1990 its fleet was one B747, two B767s, three B707s, eleven B727-200s and eleven B727-100s. In 1992 Avianca signed an extensive agreement with GPA, which enabled them to finally retire all B707s and B727-100s, and B727-200s. At the same time they could renew a large part of their fleet with leased MD-80s and B757s, plus a few B767s and retaining a single B747. For regional routes it has leased ten Fokker 50s.

EL DORADO

A small cargo operator based in Villavicencio with three DC-3s. It was founded in 1982 when it purchased four DC-3s in Canada.

One of El Dorado's DC-3s in Villavicencio in 1983. (Author's collection)

INTERANDES

This small air-taxi company operates from Bogota, mainly with light aircraft. However it does have a single DC-3 used for cargo and *ad hoc* charters. The company was originally founded in 1979.

Interandes' single DC-3 photographed in Bogota in August 1990

INTERCONTINENTAL

Intercontinental has become a major domestic airline in Colombia with thirteen DC-9s and a single Viscount (last operational in Colombia) for *ad hoc* charter. It began as *Aeropesca* in 1960, originally carrying fish and other cargo with a number of C-46s. In 1971 it acquired Viscounts from Aloha, and began a scheduled passenger service in southern Colombia. Cities served were Popayan, Pasto, Medellin, Cucuta, Barranquilla and Cali. Progress was steady during the 1970s with more Viscounts added.

In late 1982 it leased its first two DC-9-15s, and since it had long given up flying fish, it changed its name in 1983 to Intercontinental.

One of Aeropesca's C-46s with a Viscount in the background. Both caught in Bogota in 1977. The C-46 is still present at Bogota in rather poor condition. (Author's collection)

With the change of name the livery was revised to the current blue-gold. This DC-9 is seen arriving to its stand at Bogota-Eldorado airport in November 1992.

LAC

LAC, or Lineas Aereas del Caribe, is one of the bigger cargo airlines in Colombia. It was founded in 1974, initially with a C-46 but soon added DC-6Bs. It operated no less than six of these four-engined pistons before it moved up to its first DC-8 in 1980. The DC-8 has since become its main equipment, although it has also operated B707s on shorter leases.

One of its leased B707s is pictured in Miami in 1986.
(E. Gual/Aviation Photography of Miami)

LACOL

Another small cargo operator based in Villavicencio. It was founded in 1982 and currently flies two DC-3s.

HK-124 is an old-timer in the Colombian skies, having originally been delivered to Avianca in September 1947. It has since passed through a number of smaller operators. It was pictured in Bogota, November 1992.

LAP

Lineas Aereas Petroleras, as its full name reads, mainly flies for the petroleum companies, hence its name. It was founded in 1976 and has mainly flown light aircraft such as Piper Navajos and various helicopters. However it does fly a single DC-3 from its Bogota base.

LAPs' single DC-3 seen in Bogota, August 1990.

LINEAS AEREAS SURAMERICANAS

This all-cargo operator was originally founded as *Aeronorte* in 1966. Its initial aircraft were C-46s, of which one still remains. The 1970s saw a great variety of piston-engined aircraft being employed, such as DC-3s, DC-4s and a single DC-7. DC-6s and C-46s hauled its cargo during the 1980s until it suspended operations in the later part of that decade. It was subsequently relaunched as Lineas Aereas Suramericanas, and has now established itself with a couple of Caravelles, a single DC-6 and a remaining C-46. In late 1992 it took delivery of an additional Caravelle from Transwede.

Its DC-6s off-loading in Bogota in November 1992. The remaining C-46 still sporting Aeronorte titles can be seen in the background.

LINEAS AEREAS URRACA

This small airline became a well-known company within Colombia during its almost twenty-five years of operations. It was founded in 1955 by the Henao Jaramillo brothers in Villavicencio. It initially operated DC-3s which were its main equipment until 1970. In that year La Urraca bought three HP Heralds from Autair in England. Three Viscounts were also leased in November 1971. With these aircraft La Urraca entered the passenger business more seriously. However it also entered financial problems, and a number of accidents, one Viscount was lost in January 1972, and all the Heralds suffered serious accidents of one sort or another. The original owners backed out and the company was reorganized. New equipment in the shape of BN Islanders and C-46s were introduced and kept the airline going until 1979 when it ceased operations.

During the 1970s La Urraca painted its aircraft in different, bright colours. This DC-3 was photographed in Villavicencio in 1975, with another in the background.
(Jean-M. Magendie)

SAEP

SAEP is an acronym for Servicios Aereos Petroleros, and again as its name indicates it mainly flies for the oil companies in Colombia. It was founded in 1980, and mostly uses DC-3s, of which it currently has five, several bought from the Ecuadorean Air Force.

A SAEP DC-3 taxies out for take off at Bogota, November 1992. Note the letter "A" on the fin, drawn as a drilling-tower.

SAM

Sociedad Aeronautica Medellin was founded in 1945 in the city of Medellin. It bought surplus C-46s and began flying cargo within Colombia and to Miami. Initial expansion was modest, but in 1955 SAM set up a passenger airline called Rutas Aereas de Colombia together with KLM. KLM furnished an initial batch of three DC-4s. RAS began flying to Rio de Janeiro, followed by Sao Paulo and Curacao in 1960. The same year saw the introduction of DC-6B, again from KLM. However in August 1962 it went out of business, followed by SAM itself in September 1963. Avianca took over SAM and established it as a domestic scheduled passenger airline. SAM soon established a domestic network and services to neighbouring countries such as Panama and Brazil (Manaus). Four L188 Electras were purchased from Eastern in 1969. Another four followed in 1970-71. The Electras were replaced by three B720s from Avianca in 1977. The first B727-100 arrived in 1980, and this aircraft has since become the only type being employed after the 720s were retired. However, SAM is now planning to replace the B727s with Bae RJ-100s.

The current livery is shown on this B727 in Bogota, November 1992

SATENA

Like so many other South American countries, Colombia also has an airline run by the Air Force. In this case it is Satena, which stands for Servicio Aeronavegacion a Territories Nacionales. It was set up in 1962 to provide an air service to those parts of the country unserved by the commercial airlines. It began with DC-3s drawn from the air force and initially its services were not open to the public but only personnel of the government and local communities. In 1968 it became a public airline. Four new HS 748s were incorporated in 1972. During the 1970s Satena employed at least thirteen DC-3s and three DC-4s. Two 748s were lost in accidents, so another was purchased in 1981.

Two new F28-3000s were purchased in 1984 to replace the remaining DC-4s.

One of Satenas' C-212s at San Andres in February 1985.

Unfortunately one was soon lost in an accident. Six CASA 212s were added at the same time to replace the last DC-3s. Another two have since joined the fleet. Finally Satena purchased both the Pilatus Porter, and more recently Cessna Caravans for the small airfields.

TAC

Transportes Aereos del Cesar, as its full name goes, was founded in 1968 in Valledupar (El Cesar province, hence its name). Services began in January 1969 with DC-3s. However in 1971 it moved up to turbine equipment, first by acquiring two Fairchild F-27s in USA, quickly followed by three ex-Austrian Viscount 800s. Three more F-27s were acquired in 1974. TAC expanded steadily, and served by now Bogota, Barranquilla, Cartagena, Corozal and Medellin amongst other cities.

Three Caravelles were purchased in 1976 from Aviaco in Spain. Three more followed later. In January 1980 it changed its name to AeroCesar, and soon ordered two new ATR-42s for delivery 1986-87. However financial problems continued to increase and it went bankrupt in late 1982.

One of its three ex-Aviaco Caravelles in Bogota in 1976

TALA

This is a small cargo operator based in Bogota which was founded in 1983. Its full name is Transportes Aereos Latino Americanos, and it has mainly used DC-3 but also flies a single C-46.

TALAs' colourful C-46 photographed in 1984.

TAMPA

Tampa is another large cargo operator in Colombia. It was founded in 1974 with a single DC-6, with a second added in 1976. It is based in Medellin, but mainly operates out of Bogota to Miami. Its first B707 arrived in 1979, and has since operated at least eight different 707s. It also flew a leased CL-44 in the mid-1980s.

In late 1992 Tampa leased two DC-8-73s from GPA to replace its fleet of 707s.

One of Tampa's 707s taxies out for take off at Miami, March 1992. It features the current livery of Tampa.

One of its colourful DC-3s caught in
Bogota, December 1977 (ALPS)

TAXI AEREO EL VENADO

This small passenger airline was active
during the 1970s, operating from
Villavicencio. Its main equipment were
DC-3s and DC-4s plus some light aircraft.
However it did suffer a string of accidents,
and after another bad accident in 1981 it
lost its operating certificate.

ECUADOR

AECA

This fairly small cargo operator was
founded in 1980, initially operating light
aircraft from its Guayaquil base.

It moved up to heavy aircraft by leasing
a CL-44 in November 1980. After it was
returned, AECA purchased a DC-8-55F in
August 1983. However this DC-8 was lost
in a very bad accident in September 1984
when it crashed after taking off from
Quitos airport, killing sixty-five on the
ground.

To replace it, another DC-8-54 was
leased in June 1985, only to be returned in
1987 and replaced with a different
DC-8-54. After it was returned in 1991,
AECA leased a single B727-100. It recently
purchased all surviving B707s from
Ecuatoriana.

*One of AECA's leased DC-8-50s,
photographed in Quito in July 1986. The
current B727 features a red-blue cheatline.*

ANDES

Andes is the largest and oldest cargo airline in Ecuador. It was founded in 1961, and three years later began scheduled cargo flights with C-46s between Miami and Lima via Panama, Quito and Guayaquil. Between 1969 and 1970 it introduced three DC-6s, which in turn were replaced by two Canadair CC-106s in 1973-74.

In June 1977 Andes purchased its first jet-freighter, a DC-8-32 from ONA. Andes has since used a number of different DC-8s and it continues to be its only flight equipment.

One of Andes' CC-106s at a foggy Lima airport in February 1974. Notice Faucett's ramp-area in the background.

ECUATORIANA

This national airline of Ecuador was founded in 1957 by a group of local businessmen holding 81 per cent and an American, E. Heckscher holding the balance. It soon entered a cooperation with a group of airlines managed by C. N. Shelton. His main airline was TAN of Honduras. Ecuatoriana, which at this time was known as CEA (Compania Ecuatoriana de Aviacion) began flying C-46s from Guayaquil and Quito to Miami via Cali and Panama. CEA competed with Panagra by offering low fares. In 1959 it introduced its first DC-6.

The network was gradually expanded during the 1960s with more DC-6s, a few DC-4s and a single Douglas B-23. Ecuatoriana acquired its first L188 Electra in 1967, and seven more were used until phased out in 1975. By 1972 Ecuatoriana was serving Mexico City, Lima and Santiago, in addition to the original destinations. Due to its deteriorating financial situation, the government purchased 52 per cent of the shares in August 1972. However the financial problems continued, and the airline was forced to suspend operations two years later. At that moment the government nationalized the airline and introduced two ex-Pan Am B720s. A third followed in 1975. With the 720s, Ecuatoriana launched a very striking livery representing the jungles and wildlife of Ecuador. Five B707s were added between 1977 and 1981. Its network continued to expand, by 1978 Ecuatoriana also served Buenos Aires, Caracas, Los Angeles and New York.

Ecuatoriana stepped up to widebodies in 1983 when it leased an ex-Swissair DC-10-30, and soon after revised its livery to a more toned-town "rainbow" scheme.

Progress during the 1980s was fairly modest, and after lengthy evaluations, Ecuatoriana introduced two A-310s in 1992. These were aircraft originally intended for Pan Am but cancelled and could thus be obtained on good terms.

Ecuatoriana's striking livery used in the late 1970s is shown on this B720, which was purchased in 1974. (Author's collection)

SAETA

Saeta was founded in 1966 as a domestic scheduled airline. Its name is derived from "Sociedad Anonima Ecuatoriana de Transportes Aereos". Initial equipment was a Piper Aztec but it was soon joined by three DC-3s flying from Quito to Cuenca. Later Tulcan and Guayaquil were added to the network. Between 1969 and 1971 three Viscount 700s were purchased from Alitalia, however one was quickly lost in an accident in Cuenca. Saeta later bought a fourth Viscount in USA to replace it.

In 1975 Saeta purchased three SE210 Caravelles, again from Alitalia, and later another three were bought, however two of these were reduced to spares. By now Saeta was concentrating on the Quito-Guayaquil route offering up to five daily frequencies.

The 1980s were fairly steady for Saeta, a B727-100 was purchased in 1981 followed by a B707 in 1985, by which time the Caravelles had been withdrawn from service following a bad accident. With a second B727-100, Saeta began flying to Miami.

One of Saetas' B727-100s sitting on the ramp in Quito, February 1985, with a TAME Electra and SAN B-727 in the background.

A B727-200 arrived in 1991, but the big step came in 1992 when Saeta leased an A-310, mainly for its Miami route, soon followed by a second and a used B737-200. In 1994 Saeta began flying to Los Angeles.

SAN

Servicios Aereos Nacionales, as its full name goes, was founded in 1964 as an air-taxi company. Scheduled services began in 1967, again with DC-3s. It followed its rival by also buying Viscounts in 1970, however it bought the larger 800 version from ANA in Japan. Three more Viscount 700s followed in 1976-77.

Again following Saeta, SAN bought three SE210 Caravelles from TAP in Portugal in November 1975. Another two ex-Luxairs arrived in 1978. By now SAN was mainly flying the Quito-Guayaquil route in competition with Saeta and TAME. SAN bought two B727-100s in 1981, however one was sold to Danair the following year.

The ownership of SAN and Saeta merged during the early 1980s, thus the two companies were controlled by the same owner, but continued to operate separately. SAN continued with its single B727, while Saeta expanded its fleet and network.

The single B727-100 comes in for landing at Quito, December 1988. It features the current colour scheme.

TAME

TAME was set up by the Ecuadorean Air Force in 1962 to operate a domestic scheduled passenger service. Operations began immediately with two DC-3s flying between Quito and Guayaquil. TAME soon established a more extensive domestic network, and with the introduction of DC-6s in 1967, it launched a scheduled air service to the Galapagos Islands.

In 1970 TAME acquired, through the Air Force, brand new HS-748s which still remain the aircraft used for regional routes. The DC-6s remained on the trunk routes until replaced by four Electras in 1974-75. During the 1970s, TAME was serving Tulcan, Manta, Portoviejo, Cuenca, Quito, Guayaquil, Machala and Macara.

In 1980, TAME purchased its first jet aircraft, a brand new B727-200 from Boeing, followed by a new B737 in 1981. However the 737 was lost in an accident in Cuenca in 1983, instead TAME bought three used B727-100s from Philippine Airlines in 1984-85. At the same time a new F28-4000 was ordered, mainly for the service to Loja. By now the Electras had been virtually grounded, hence TAME did an unusual exchange with Varig, by giving Varig two Electras, Varig agreed to overhaul and repaint the remaining two in 1986. By now the network had grown to include Lago Agrio, Tarapoa, Coca and Macas all in the Amazon region.

In 1992 TAME bought a B727 from Lufthansa, and at the same time agreed to feed Lufthansas flights in Caracas, by connecting from Quito via Bogota.

A TAME Electra coming in to land at Quito, December 1988. This was TAME's last operational Electra, mainly used for the Amazon destinations. It was unfortunately lost in an accident soon afterwards, thus ending the Electra operations in Ecuador after twenty-one years.

PARAGUAY

LAP

Lineas Aereas Paraguayas, or LAP, as it is more commonly referred to, is the national state-owned airline of Paraguay which was founded in 1962. It began operations with

three ex-Aerolineas CV-240 in August the following year when it began flying from Asuncion to Buenos Aires and Sao Paulo/Rio de Janeiro. Santa Cruz in Bolivia was soon added to the network. One

CV-240 was lost in an accident at Ezeiza airport in Buenos Aires in May 1967. To replace the two surviving Convairs, LAP acquired three L188 Electras from Eastern in 1969, and these were to remain in operations for over 20 years. The early 1970s saw Lima, Peru and Resistencia, Argentina being added, Resistencia was served with a single DC-3 leased from the Air Force, however the route did not last for long.

The next acquisition came in 1978 when LAP purchased two ex-Pan Am B-707s. In the same year LAP extended the Lima route to Miami. A third B-707 followed two years later.

The big route extension came in 1979 when LAP began flying twice a week to Europe (Madrid & Frankfurt).

In 1984 and 1988 LAP incorporated two DC-8-60s, partially replacing the B-707s. Only one L188 was by then still in service, mainly flying to Santa Cruz. LAP entered the widebody era in 1992 with a lease of a single DC-10-30. The government announced its intention to privatize the airline, but it lost substantial amounts and ceased operations in early 1994.

The Electra was the backbone of LAPs' fleet during the 1970s, and remained in service until recently. ZP-CBZ was the last operational Electra, it was photographed in Asuncion in November 1984.

LAPs' first DC-8 arrived in 1984, it was ZP-CCH which is seen preparing for departure at Ezeiza airport in Buenos Aires, April 1985.

TAM

TAM is the domestic airline of Paraguay, and it is operated by the Air Force using their equipment. For many years TAM relied on DC-3s seconded from the Air Force. Amongst the domestic points served are Pilar, Filadelfia, Encarnacion, Bahia Negra, Olimpo, and Pto Pres. Stroessner. The DC-3s were partially replaced by four CASA 212s in 1984.

One of TAM's C212s at Asuncion, November 1984.

PERU

AEROICA

This small air-taxi operator was founded in 1978. Its main business is taking tourists down to the famous Nazca archaeological site.

Amongst the light aircraft it employed was this DH Beaver, photographed in Nazca, November 1984. It was later lost in an incident.

AEROCARGA PERUANA

This small cargo airline was founded in 1982 with a single DC-8-55F. However the aircraft was soon parked in Lima, and eventually ended up with Faucett.

Aerocargo's only DC-8 seen at Smyrna, TN, before delivery, May 1982.

AMERICANA DE AVIACION

This was another domestic airline set up after the deregulation. It leased three B727s in 1991, some of these coming from another domestic airline which had gone bankrupt, namely Aerochasqui.

An Americana B727 at Lima-Chavez airport, No. (Tony Härry)

ANDREA

This small domestic airline was set up after Peru deregulated its domestic air services. The intention was to lease three F28s from Linjeflyg in Sweden. The first arrived in July 1991, followed by the second in September. Before the third could be delivered the airline went bankrupt, both F28s returning to Linjeflyg between December 1991 and January 1992 after only a few months of operations.

The F-28s were operated all-white with titles only, and were never registered in Peru. SE-DGC was photographed in Stockholm after its return from Peru. (T. Lakmaker)

APSA

Aerolineas Peruanas SA, or APSA as it was more commonly known, was founded in September 1956. It began operations in June the following year with a C-46 on the Lima-Antofagasta-Santiago route. One month later the network was extended north to Managua and Tegucigalpa, thus connecting with TAN of Honduras. The joint backer of these two airlines was C. N. Shelton who could thus circumvent bilateral agreements by establishing associate airlines in different countries. With the same logic he was behind the foundation of CEA in Ecuador. In 1958 the southern route was extended to Buenos Aires, and in 1960 APSA began services to Miami via Panama using DC-6s. Meanwhile APSA ordered two new L188 Electras, only to later cancel the order. Instead APSA opted for the CV-990 by leasing one in 1963, followed by two more in 1965 and 1968. A single DC-7B was also flown between 1965 and 1968. Meanwhile the network expanded, La Paz, Rio de Janeiro, Asuncion and Montevideo being added in 1964. Mexico and Los Angeles followed in 1966, and finally APSA took the step across the Atlantic, by starting services to London, Madrid and Paris in 1969. For this purpose APSA leased a

DC-8 from Iberia, followed by a second in 1970. However, the tremendous expansion had a price, APSA started accumulating huge losses, and abruptly suspended operations on 3rd May, 1971. Its three CV-990s and two DC-8s were repossessed by the owners.

One of APSAs' three CV-990s stored in Tucson, it never flew again, and is still stored in Marana. (Author's collection)

AERONAVES DEL PERU

This all-cargo airline began operations in November 1965 with three DC-6s. Initially Aeronaves carried passengers, but it went all-cargo in 1971. A single DC-7CF was added in December 1969 followed by two CL-44s in 1975. After briefly flying an L-188 Electra in 1977-78, Aeronaves acquired its first jet aircraft, a DC-8-43 in November 1978. Like Aeroperu, Aeronaves

were to standardize on the DC-8 in the future, with another seven DC-8s arriving between 1980 and 1983.

In 1982 the owners of Aeronaves purchased 59 per cent of Faucett, but the two airlines continued as separate companies. A couple of DC-8s were transferred over to Faucett.

Aeronaves has lately operated a few B707s, this aircraft arrived in 1990 and is still in use. It was photographed in Miami in June 1990.
(Aviation Photography of Miami/E.Gual)

AEROPERU

After APSAs bankruptcy, Peru was left without an international airline of its own. Thus the government decided to reorganize a domestic airline run by the air force, SATCO, as the new national airline of Peru. Hence Aeroperu was formed on 22nd May, 1973 with three ex-SATCO F28-1000s. The first international route began on 28th July, 1974 to Buenos Aires via Santiago. At the same time it began flying to Guayaquil. In September this route was extended to Miami. A year later Los Angeles was added. Finally New York, Caracas and Bogota was inaugurated in 1978.

Fleetwise, Aeroperu absorbed the three F28s, and bought a B727-100 from Eastern. For the domestic side, an F-27 was leased from Maersk, prior to the delivery of two new F27s in 1975. The long-haul routes were flown by DC-8-50s leased from KLM, Air Jamaica and Viasa. Another B727-100 was bought from Lufthansa in 1978 followed by two B727-200s from Cruzeiro in 1983. Meanwhile, Aeroperu had attempted its first widebody, by leasing two ex-PSA L-1011 Tristars in 1978 to open the New York route, these were however returned to Lockheed four years later as Aeroperu acquired more DC-8s from Alitalia and SAS.

The 1980s were fairly uneventful, the F-27s being phased out. In 1990 Aeroperu leased a B767 from Britannia for six months. A year later it attempted to operate an L-1011 jointly with Faucett but it did not last long. Meanwhile Aeroperu was losing money and the government decided to privatize it. After inviting bids for the airline, Aeromexico was declared the new owner of Aeroperu in early 1993.

Aeromexico introduced DC-10-30s and B727-200 featuring a livery very similar to its own.

By the late 1970s Aeroperu had adopted this livery, as shown on one of their F28s at Lima in November 1984.

A Faucett BAC-111 at the ramp in Lima, July 1977. In the background is the Faucett maintenance area with four DC-6s, one DC-4 and one DC-3. They feature the livery used during the 1960s and 1970s.

FAUCETT

The oldest of all airlines in Peru is Faucett, which was founded in 1928 by a local group of business people led by an American, Elmer Faucett, who gave his name to the airline. Operations began in September 1928 from Lima to Chiclayo, soon extending to Arequipa in the south and Talara in the north. Initial equipment was Stinson Detroiter. Faucett later developed its own aircraft, the Faucett F-19 from a Stinson design and produced it in Peru. It first flew in 1934, and twelve were built. Faucett steadily developed its domestic network, and by 1946 it served over twenty-five destinations, with its F-19s. In the early postwar years Faucett introduced a large number of DC-3s, followed in 1950 by its first DC-4, of which it purchased eight. The first DC-6B was introduced in 1960. Meanwhile Panagra had acquired 20 per cent, which was passed to Braniff when it took over Panagra in 1967. Faucett received a permit to start flying internationally in 1960 but it decided to stay on the domestic scene. International cargo flights began in 1970.

After six DC-6Bs were bought during the 1960s Faucett upgraded to jets, by introducing a new B727-100 in 1968. Two new BAC-111-475s of the special "hot and high" version were purchased in 1971. During the 1970s Faucett leased various B727s, plus purchasing a third BAC-111. The last pistons were retired in the late 1970s and the remaining DC-4s and DC-6s were sold, after some time in storage, to Bolivia in 1981. However, Faucett's financial situation deteriorated, the three BAC-111s were repossessed by Bae in 1982, at the same time Aeronaves del Peru bought 59 per cent of the company. Aeronaves transferred some DC-8s. During the 1980s Faucett continued leasing aircraft on fairly short terms, mainly B737s and B727s. It did finally expand into the international arena, by beginning services to Miami. Lately it has leased two L-1011 Tristars for this route. It unsuccessfully bid to buy Aeroperu in 1992-93.

One of its DC-8s featuring the livery used in the 1980s photo taken in February 1985 in Lima. Faucett has recently gone back to its previous livery, although many leased aircraft are flown all-white with titles only.

PERUANA

A small domestic airline operating Russian equipment, mainly two leased AN-12s plus light aircraft, later ceased operations.

One of Peruana's two AN-12s at Lima, November 1991, still in basic Aeroflot livery. (Tony Härry)

SURINAM

SURINAM AIRWAYS

When Surinam gained its independence from the Netherlands it quickly reorganized its airline as "Surinam Airways", and with leased DC-8s began flying to Amsterdam. It later added Miami, Manaus and Belem.

Airline operations in Surinam go back to 1954 when SLM, Surinaamse Luchtvaart Maatschappij, was founded by the Dutch colonial government. During the 1960s it flew various services in cooperation with ALM.

Surinam currently operates a single DC-8-63 for the international routes and two Twin Otters for the domestic network.

Surinam Airways' DC-8 at Miami, April 1986. Surinam has leased various DC-8s during the 1980s.

URUGUAY

AEROLINEAS URUGUAYAS

This small all-cargo airline began operations in 1990 with a single B-707, mainly flying to USA from Montevideo.

Aerolineas Uruguayas' single B-707 seen taking off from Miami, March 1992.

AEROSUR

Aerosur is another all-cargo airline based in Montevideo. It operates a single B-707 which it acquired in August 1990.

Aerosur's single B-707 also taking off from Miami, November 1991.

AERO URUGUAY

It began as an all-freight airline in 1977 with the assistance of Cargolux. After briefly using a CL-44 it introduced its own B-707 in 1978 on cargo flights to USA and Europe. After briefly using a DC-8-63 it ceased operations in 1982.

It restarted operations in 1986 with a leased DC-8-55F. The following year it entered the Colonia-Buenos Aires passenger market with a single F-27, after ARCO ceased operations. The DC-8 was later replaced by a B-707, and an FH-227 was added in 1992.

Aero Uruguay's F-27 taking off from Buenos Aires-Aeroparque in November 1988. It still carries parts of the Horizon livery, as this F-27 was purchased from De Havilland, who in turn had taken it from Horizon as a trade-in for new DHC-8s.

One of ARCO's CV-240s climbing away from Aeroparque, in 1974.

ARCO

ARCO, or Aerolineas Colonia SA, as its full name goes, was founded in 1957. Principal shareholder was a bus company called ONDA. It began operations in 1964 on the Colonia-Buenos Aires route with three C-46s. ONDA connected with a bus service from Colonia to Montevideo and could thus offer a much lower fare than Aerolineas and Pluna flying directly between the two capitals.

Three CV-240s were purchased in the early 1970s to replace the C-46s. These in turn were replaced by two CV-600s, one arriving in 1976, the other in 1981.

However ARCO ceased operations in December 1986, and was declared bankrupt during spring 1987. Aero Uruguay soon replaced it on the Colonia market.

ARCO's CV-600 caught at Aeroparque, December 1976.

PLUNA

The national airline of Uruguay is Pluna, which stands for Primeras Lineas Uruguayas de Navegacion Aerea. Pluna was founded in 1935, and began operations the following year with two DH Dragonflies. After getting some government subsidies Pluna introduced the larger DH.86B in 1937. After the government decided against buying 49 per cent of Pluna in 1943, it ceased operations. It resumed services in September 1945, now with 83 per cent of the shares held by the government. Its fleet was then DC-2s and DC-3s. Up to now the airline only flew domestic services, but in 1948 Pluna opened its first international route to Porto Alegre in Brazil. After the government bought the remaining shares of Pluna, in 1951, it ordered four new DH Herons and began flying to Asuncion in Paraguay. In 1956 it entered the highly competitive Montevideo-Buenos Aires market. Pluna continued its tradition of buying British, when it introduced three new Viscount 700s in 1958. In the same year the four Herons were sold in England. Two more ex-Alitalia Viscounts were added in 1967. Meanwhile it had extended its northern route system to Sao Paulo and Rio de Janeiro.

Pluna acquired its first jet aircraft in December 1969 when a single B737 was delivered new from the factory. However, the early 1970s proved difficult, Pluna was reorganized so that the domestic network was taken over by the Uruguay Air Force (flying as TAMU), and the single 737 was sold in 1974 to TAN in Honduras. Instead three second-hand Viscount 800s were purchased from VASP in Brazil.

After briefly using two ex-Lufthansa B727-100s, Pluna acquired three brand new B737s in 1982. At the same time it

entered an agreement with Transavia, whereby Transavia would lease one B737 every year in the summer with peak charter traffic, which coincides with the winter in Uruguay which is the low season.

With an ex-Aerolineas B707 Pluna began flying to Europe (Madrid) in the early 1980s. During this decade Pluna leased several B707s from Aerolineas and DC-8s in USA for its Atlantic operation. By the early 1990s Pluna was reported as studying the possibility of acquiring widebodies, but meanwhile the government announced its intention to privatize the airline, hence no widebodies have arrived yet.

One of the Viscount 800s arriving at Buenos Aires "downtown" Aeroparque airport, December 1976. It displays the livery used by Pluna from the 1950s until the arrival of the B-737. However, Pluna briefly used a bright orange colour scheme on its first 737 and one Viscount.

This B737 taxying out at Aeroparque in April 1985, shows Pluna's current livery.

TAMU

Transportes Aereos Militares Uruguayos, or simply TAMU, assumed Pluna's domestic network in the early 1970s. It is operated by the Uruguay Air Force using their equipment. Initially it relied mainly on DC-3s, but then F-27s, E-110 Bandeirantes and CASA 212s were used. TAMU also operated the Montevideo-Buenos Aires route during the mid 1970s, using its F-27 and FH227 aircraft.

TAMUs' FH227 climbing away from Aeroparque, December 1976. Notice how the aircraft carries both a military serial, "T-570", and a civilian registration, CX-BHX.

VENEZUELA

AEROEJECUTIVOS

This small cargo and *ad hoc* charter airline has been operating DC-3s since the early 1980s. With bases at Caracas-Maiquetia airport and the general aviation airport ,"Aeropuerto de Caracas", it has mainly used DC-3s, but in the last couple of years has also operated two DC-6s. Sadly one of these was lost in an accident off Curacao recently.

One of several DC-3s employed by Aeroejecutivos, this one was photographed in Caracas-Maiquetia, November 1992.

AEROPOSTAL

Aeropostal or LAV, standing for Linea Aeropostal Venezolana, can trace its origins to 1929 when the French Aeropostal set up a Venezuelan subsidiary. Operations began the following year from Maracaibo to Maracay and on to Ciudad Bolivar, Guasipati and Tumeremo in the east. In 1931 this route was extended to Trinidad. Initial equipment used were Latecoere 26 and 28s. On 31st December, 1933 the Venezuelan government bought the whole operation. It was reorganized in 1935 as "Linea Aeropostal Venezolana". Three Fairchild 71s replaced the French aircraft in 1937 followed by Lockheed 10 Electras in 1938. Later it purchased Lockheeds 14s. LAV expanded its domestic network during the war and in 1945 it launched international routes, first to Boa Vista in Brazil with Aruba and Bogota following in 1946. By now LAV served twenty-five domestic destinations, mostly in competition with Avensa. DC-3s started arriving in 1946, and LAV operated at least twenty-four of these until the mid-1970s. LAV also acquired two new L-049 Constellations in 1946 for its route to New York which was inaugurated in March 1947. Another two L-749s arrived in the same year. The early 1950s saw the arrival of two Martin 202s and several C-46s. In 1953 LAV began flying across the Atlantic to Rome, Lisbon and Madrid. Three years later LAV took delivery of three new Viscount 700s. When LAV assisted in the formation of Viasa, in 1961, they withdrew from the international routes. Six HS-748s arrived in 1965 for the regional routes. In 1968 the first of many DC-9s arrived, and LAV came to operate all versions, the -15s, -32s, 51s and MD-80s. Meanwhile, in 1977, LAV acquired six new DH Twin Otters for regional services in the southern part of Venzeuela. However, this whole operation was later sold to Aerotuy. LAV also returned to the international arena by starting services to Port of Spain, Aruba, Curacao, and San Juan. By 1992 LAV had a fleet of six MD-83s, seven DC-9-51s, three DC-9-30s and one DC-9-15. By now the airline simply called itself "Aeropostal" although the abbreviation "LAV" is occasionally used.

One of Aeropostal's DC-9-50s at Caracas in 1977, showing the livery used in the late 1970s and most of the 1980s. During the early 1970s Aeropostal used a lilac livery. The Venezuelan government is currently trying to privatize Aeropostal.

This MD-80 shows the modified livery currently used. Photograph taken in Caracas, September 1992.

AVENSA

This private Venezuelan carrier was founded on 13th May, 1943 by Henry L. Boulton and Pan Am who took 30 per cent of the shares. Freight operations began in December 1943. In 1944 the shareholding was changed, Pan Am reduced its share to 23 per cent, Boulton took 31 per cent, with the rest split amongst other shareholders. Fleet at this time was three Ford Trimotors, one Stinson Reliant and one Lockheed 12. A passenger service between Caracas and Ciudad Bolivar began. In 1946 Pan Am increased its share to 37 per cent, and DC-3s were introduced. In 1953 the first CV-340 arrived. These Convair twins were to remain with Avensa for over thirty-five years, although they were converted to CV-580s in the 1960s.

In November 1954 Avensa got the permission to start flying to Miami, and this route was inaugurated in June 1955. Avensa remained an international carrier until Viasa was founded in 1961. In 1958 Avensa acquired two DC-6Bs from Pan Am and five new Fairchild F-27s. However, the F-27s were fairly short-lived, being sold in 1963.

Avensa moved to jets in 1964 when it bought a single Caravelle from Varig. Three years later it acquired two new DC-9-14s. By now Avensa had developed an extensive domestic network in competition with LAV. By 1967 it served twenty-three domestic destinations with a fleet of one Caravelle, two DC-9s and a large fleet of Convairs and a few DC-3s.

In the 1970s Avensa bought many DC-9s on the second-hand market, unfortunately it lost its only Caravelle in an accident in

1973. Several DC-9s were later transferred to its American leasing branch which then leased the aircraft to various US operators.

In 1979 Avensa introduced its first two B727s, and this tri-jet was to form the backbone of the fleet during the 1980s, while most DC-9s were either sold or leased. A few CV-580s were retained for regional routes.

The early 1990s saw a reversal of this policy, most 727s were sold, many to TAESA in Mexico, while Avensa bought a number of DC-9-30s and -50s in the US, mainly ex-Eastern and Midway aircraft. At the same time it created a subsidiary called "Servivensa" to handle both domestic and international routes. Avensa and Servivensa re-entered the international arena by starting flights to New York, Miami, Bogota, Panama and San Jose amongst others. Two B-757s were leased for its international network.

When Servivensa was created, Avensa once again looked to Pan Am for ideas, creating a livery very similar to the one used by Pan Am in the 1950s. This B727 is about to touch down at Miami, May 1992.

CAVE

This small regional airline was founded in 1987, initially operating light aircraft. It acquired three BN Trilanders in Panama, and three used Metro IIs. It operated a scheduled air service from Caracas-Maiquetia airport. However, in late 1993 it suspended operations.

One of CAVE's Metro IIs taxying out for take off at Maiquetia, September 1992.

One of three C-46s that were left at Caracas-Maiquetia airport for many years until scrapped. This photo was taken in November 1984.

LATIN CARGA

This small all-cargo airline was operating C-46s during the early 1970s, at least six passing through its hands. In December 1975 Latin Carga leased a single DC-6B which was returned one year later. It also briefly used a DC-7 from the same source, before it added a single CV-880 in 1978. By now the C-46s had been taken out of service and the CV-880 was its only equipment. When it crashed in November 1980, after take off from Caracas, losing power on several engines, the airline ceased operations.

RENTAVION

This small non-scheduled passenger airline began operations in the late 1980s with two DC-3s and a single Martin 404. However, by 1992 the M-404 seemed to be mostly parked at Maiquetia airport.

Rentavion's single M-404 at Maiquetia, November 1992.

RUTACA

This small operator based in Ciudad Bolivar has been operating DC-3s and light aircraft for many years. Recently it has acquired two EMB-110s for scheduled passenger service, plus a couple of AN-2s for air-taxi work.

One of several active DC-3s in the Rutaca fleet. Photo taken at Ciudad Bolivar, November 1992. (T. Lakmaker)

VIASA

Viasa is Venezuela's main international carrier, being formed by LAV and Avensa in November 1960. The following year it entered a cooperation with KLM, in which KLM became the European agent and leased aircraft to Viasa. Viasa ordered two new CV-880s, meanwhile it began operations with a leased DC-8 from KLM on 1st April, 1961. It soon began operations to New York, Miami and Bogota. The two CV-880s were delivered August-September 1961, a third following in 1963. During the 1960s Viasa leased two DC-9-10s for services to the Caribbean in cooperation with Dominicana and PAISA.

In 1966 Viasa took delivery of two new DC-8-53s, followed by two DC-8-63s two years later. Other DC-8s were leased during the 1970s.

In 1968 Viasa created a separate cargo airline called Transcarga which began operating an all-cargo DC-8.

In April 1972 Viasa ordered two DC-10-30s, these entering service in April

1974. Viasa also operated various leased B747s in the early 1980s.

Viasa entered the 1990s with five DC-10-30s and two A300s, which had been purchased in 1987 from Lufthansa. At the same time the Venezuelan government decided to privatize the airline. KLM and Iberia competed in the bidding, which Iberia won in August 1991 when it

purchased 60 per cent of the airline. For the local services, Iberia later transferred four B727-200s to Viasa.

One of Viasa's DC-10s in Panama, February 1985.

ZULIANA DE AVIACION

This international airline was set up in 1985 in Maracaibo, initially flying cargo but later it began a scheduled passenger service with B727-200s. Its name is derived from the state of Zulia.

One of Zuilana's B727s at Miami, one of its regular destinations, July 1992.

CARIBBEAN AIRLINES

AEROCHAGO

This airline initially began operating under the name "Aeromar", using C-46s on cargo flights from Santo Domingo. In the early 1980s it also leased in B-707s and DC-8s, mainly for its flights to Miami. Around 1983 it changed its operating name to Aerochago, and at the same time began a long association with Constellations, currently having two L.1049 Constellations operational along with a single DC-7. A CV-240 was used in the mid-1980s but was lost in an accident. Its only DC-6 has recently appeared with Aeromar titles, but it is not clear whether this is a separate airline or simply a different name being employed.

L-749 HI-422 taxying in at San Juan in November 1985. It was originally delivered to TWA in 1951, however it no longer remains in service having been replaced by two L-1049s.

AEROVIAS QUISQUEYANA

This airline was founded in 1962 in the Dominican Republic. Its main activity has been cargo operations. For many it has been well known for its Constellation operations, although it also operates B-707s.

One of Quisqueyana's Constellations in Santo Domingo, 1978. This aircraft was sold to TRADO in 1979 and used for spares. (D. Hagedorn)

ABC COMMUTER

ABC was set up in 1981 to handle local flights between Curacao, Aruba and Bonaire on behalf of ALM. For this purpose it purchased two new DH Twin Otters. In 1990 it was merged with ALM, and the Twin Otters replaced by the FH-227s.

DH Twin Otter PJ-TOA at its home base of Curacao, January 1987.

Aerotours' B707 caught in Santo Domingo, November 1985.

AEROTOURS

Aerotours was founded in 1973 and began operations the following year with Constellations, initially flying passengers on non-scheduled flights. Later it mainly flew cargo within the Caribbean and to Central America, from its base in Santo Domingo. Its Constellations were in service until the early 1980s when they were replaced by B-707 aircraft. It also briefly used a Caravelle before ceasing operations in 1989.

AERO VIRGIN ISLANDS

This scheduled passenger airline was founded in 1977 in St. Thomas. Its main service was from the US Virgin Islands to San Juan, Puerto Rico. For most of its existence it relied on DC-3s, including buying the whole DC-3 fleet from Air BVI when they switched to HS 748s. However increasing competition and finally the hurricane of 1989 forced the airline out of business, although it did introduced a Martin 404 briefly before it ceased operations.

One of its DC-3s in San Juan, January 1986.

AIR ARUBA (FQ)

When Aruba became independent, Air Aruba was set up in September 1986 as the national airline by local business interests and Air Holland. It began operations in August 1988, initially operating two YS-11s. A B-757 was leased from Air Holland in April 1990 for the longer routes and later a third YS-11 was added for local services. Air Aruba has since operated various aircraft on short leases, its current fleet consisting of a B-767 leased from Air New Zealand, two MD-80s from Polaris plus a single E-120 for local services.

After Air Holland's demise, these shares were picked up by the local shareholders making Air Aruba a locally owned airline.

AIR BVI (BL)

This local airline of British Virgin Islands began operations in August 1971 with BN Islanders. DC-3s were added to the fleet late in 1975. HS.748s leased from Danair replaced the DC-3s during 1985. The airline was owned by local business interests.

Air BVI flew mainly from Tortola to San Juan but also served other destinations within the British and US Virgin Islands. However, by the early 1990s local competition increased consequently Air BVI went bankrupt during the summer of 1991. At the time of its demise it operated three 748s and three Islanders.

DC-3 VP-LVM being stored at San Juan after its withdrawal from service.

Air Aruba's single E-120 at Aruba airport, July 1992.

HS-748 VP-LVO still sporting basic Danair livery at Tortola/Beef Island in November 1985.

AIR GUADELOUPE

This regional airline was set up in 1970 by Air France and the local government of Guadeloupe to provide a scheduled air service from Pointe-a-Pitre. It initially employed BN2A Islander and Twin Otters, and later added F-27s. Today its fleet consists of two ATR-42s, two DHC-6s, and three D0-228s. A DC-10 is leased from Minerve to fly to Paris in cooperation with Air Martinique. The airline flies about 550,000 passengers a year.

One of two Fairchild F-27s employed by Air Guadeloupe during the 1980s, F-OGJC is seen at Pointe-a-Pitre, January 1985.

AIR HAITI

Air Haiti was set up in December 1969 and began cargo operations the following year. Flying B707 and C-46 aircraft, its main base was Port-au-Prince

One of Air Haiti´s C-46s coming in to land in Miami, 1980. (Author's collection)

AIR JAMAICA   (JM)

During the 1940s and 1950s a local air service was provided by BWIA. However, in August 1963, Jamaica set up its own local airline, namely Air Jamaica, with BWIA holding 16 per cent of the shares, BOAC/Cunard 33 per cent and the balance held by the Jamaican government. Services did not start until 1966. In 1968 the airline was completely reorganized with Air Canada assuming 40 per cent of the shares, and the Jamaican government the rest. Initial equipment consisted of two ex-Air Canada DC-9-30s, later supplemented by various DC-8s. During the early 1970s Air Jamaica steadily added new destinations in the USA and Europe. The Air Canada shareholding was gradually reduced to zero. In the mid-1970s four B727-200s had joined the fleet. In 1983 it incorporated two ex-Laker A300s, having by this time phased out the DC-9s and DC-8s. The current fleet is four A300s and four B-727-200s.

One of Air Jamaica´s B-727s at Kingston's International airport, June 1992.

AIR MARTINIQUE

It was originally founded in 1964 to operate a scheduled air service linking Fort de France with Barbados and Dominica. However, after it ceased operations a new Air Martinique was set up on 25th July, 1981 with local interests owning 40 per cent and Euralair and Air Affaires Int the balance. It initially used DHC-6 Twin Otter and Beech 99 but these were later replaced by two ATR-42s and three Do-228s. It carries about 35,000 passengers a year. For the future it is planning to introduce a B-737-300 in cooperation with Air Guadeloupe.

Do-228 F-OGOZ taxying in at St.Vincent, July 1992.

AIR SAINT BARTH

This local airline is based on the island of Saint Barthelemy and operates a Twin Otter, Do-228, and Trislander to neighbouring islands.

Its single Twin Otter coming in to land at St. Maarten, one of its principal destinations, February 1992.

AIR ANGUILLA

This small island, still a UK dependent territory, in the Leeward Islands chain sports its own airline. Air Anguilla flies two BN Islanders and two DHC Twin Otters on regional routes from Anguilla.

One of Air Anguilla's Twin Otters in San Juan, November 1992.

ALM

ALM can trace its origin to the KLM West Indies division set up in Curacao in 1935 with Fokker F.XVIII and F.VIII aircraft. In 1938 Lockheed 14s joined the fleet. This division became unique in operating the DC-5 from 1950 although its stay was short. Instead the postwar period saw DC-3s and DC-4s being employed, supplemented by CV-340s in 1954.

With a fleet of CV-340s, ALM (Antilliaanse Luchtvaart Maatschappij) was formed as a separate division of KLM on 1st August, 1964. On 1st January, 1969 ALM became an independent carrier. At this time ALM employed F-27s and DC-9-15s. The DC-9-15s where replaced by DC-9-32s in 1975, which in turn were replaced by the current MD-82s in 1982.

On the turboprop end ALM purchased two FH-227s from DAT but these were soon replaced by DHC-8-300s. An L188 Electra is currently leased for all-cargo flights.

From its base in Curacao, ALM serves Miami and Atlanta in the US, plus various points in the Caribbean, Venezuela, Guyana and Surinam.

KLM has recently purchased 40 per cent of ALM, the balance being still owned by the local government.

MD-82 PJ-SEG approaching Miami in May 1992, still features the older ALM livery.

One of Air Mar Freight Systems' C-46s at San Juan in November 1985.

AMSA

Aerolineas Mundo SA, or AMSA as it usually calls itself, was founded in 1986 out of "Air Mar Freight Systems". This airline began operations in the early 1980s with the two C-46s based in San Juan. Once AMSA was founded it moved its base to Santo Domingo, and incorporated Constellations as wells as two C-46s. However its two Constellations have not survived, one crashed in the sea off Puerto Rico, and the other was damaged by a DC-4 in Borinquen. Instead AMSA has switched to DC-7s and currently operates three, in addition to the two C-46s.

AMSA has recently introduced DC-7s. This is one of two immaculate aircraft on the Dominican register, a third is registered in Honduras. HI-621CT is seen loading at a crowded ramp in Santo Domingo in November 1992.

ANTILLAS AIR CARGO

This newcomer to the cargo scene in the Dominican Republic uses a C-46 for cargo runs, mainly to Puerto Rico. In 1991 it also joined the small band of airlines who still use the DC-7, when it added a single DC-7 to its fleet.

Antillas' DC-7 shortly after it joined the fleet, Miami, December 1991. This DC-7 crashed into the sea after take off from Miami, on 5th November, 1992.

ARGO SA

This cargo airline in the Dominican Republic was founded in 1971, and began operations with C-46s. It acquired an L-749 Constellation in 1979 which was lost in an accident, however it was quickly replaced by another. By the late 1980s the airline had ceased operations and its single L-749 now sits in Santo Domingo.

L-749 HI-328 was lost in an accident off St.Thomas in October 1981. It is pictured here the year prior to its accident.
(E. Gual/Aviation Photography of Miami)

One of Bahamasair's B-737s climbing out from Miami, February 1986.

BAHAMASAIR

Bahamasair was set up in June 1973 with the government assuming a majority shareholding. It took over from Out Island Airways and Flamingo Airlines. Initial equipment was BAC-111s, FH-227s and Twin Otters. In 1979 it purchased four new Bae.748-2Bs to replace the FH-227s. These aircraft were mainly used for the extensive domestic operation but also served Miami, West Palm Beach and Ft. Lauderdale. They were in turn replaced by DHC-8-300s. In the early 1980s the BAC-111s were gradually replaced by B-737s with Bahamasair eventually operating four of these aircraft until they discontinued jet operations in 1991 and only flew the DHC-8-300s both domestically and to Florida. This was the result of mounting losses due to stiff competition from the US carriers. Since then Bahamasair has leased A320s for its US destinations.

The 748s were mainly used on the domestic network. This 748 is seen on a scheduled stop at Deadmans Cay, Bahamas, November 1985.

BORINQUEN AIR

This all-cargo airline in Puerto Rico has been in business since 1961. During the 1980s it mainly used three DC-3s (one of which used the name Air Puerto Rico), but after two accidents this fleet has been reduced to a single aircraft. The survivor has been sold to Delta to be restored to its original condition, and in the future Borinquen will rely on two Beech 18s.

N28PR caught in San Juan in September 1985. This particular DC-3 was later lost in an accident.

BRITISH CARIBBEAN AIRWAYS

This airline was formed early in 1986 to offer a direct air service from Tortola to Miami, instead of having to change aircraft in San Juan. Operations began in March with a single Bae.146-100 leased from Bae. The intention was to operate two of these aircraft, but traffic developments did not follow the projections and the airline went bankrupt in October the same year. The single 146 was repossessed by Bae on 12th October, 1986.

Its single Bae.146 N246SS in Miami, April 1986.

BWIA

BWIA, or British West Indian Airways as its full name reads, was set up in 1939 by the New Zealander, Lowell Yerex, who had earlier established TACA in Central America. With a single Lodestar it began operations the following year. Lowell Yerex's interest in the airline soon disappeared, and instead local owners together with the Trinidad government and BOAC assumed control. BWIA rapidly extended its network across the Caribbean. During the 1950s BWIA went through various ownerships and route changes. Viscounts were introduced in 1955. In

Tristar 500 N314OD at St. Lucia International airport in July, 1992.

November 1961 the Trinidad government assumed 90 per cent control with BOAC the remaining 10 per cent. In 1963 BWIA introduced B727s, later to be followed by B707s. BOAC sold its share in 1967 to the Trinidad government.

BWIA currently flies to USA (New York & Miami), Canada (Toronto), Europe (London, Frankfurt, Zurich & Stockholm), Venezuela (Caracas), Guyana (Georgetown) and within the Caribbean using a fleet of MD-80s and four Tristar 500s.

CARIBBEAN AIR CARGO

This all-cargo airline based in Barbados began operations in 1980 with a single B-707 aircraft, which was soon joined by a second B-707. Its two B-707s were sold in 1989, and after this it leased equipment on an *ad hoc* basis.

One of its two B-707 during a regular visit to Miami, May 1986.
(E. Gual/Aviation Photography of Miami)

CARIB-WEST AIRWAYS

Carib-West Airways was formed in 1971 to provide cargo services from Barbados throughout the Caribbean. Initial equipment consisted of DC-3s, later it used leased C-46s and DC-4s. By the early 1980s it had ceased operations.

Carib West´s DC-3 8P-AAA at Barbados, January 1974. This aircraft was later used for spares by Tropic Air, and finally broken up.

CARIBBEAN AIR SERVICE (CASAIR)

Caribbean Air Service was set up in 1962 as Virgin Island Airways. Its main activity was cargo with C-46s from St. Croix to San Juan, Miami, St. Lucia, Antigua, Guadeloupe, St. Kitts and St. Maarten. By the early 1980s it had ceased operations

One of Casair´s C-46s, withdrawn from use at San Juan, November 1985. It has since been scrapped.

CARIBBEAN UNITED

Originally formed as Arawak Airlines in June 1970 in Trinidad, this company changed its name in 1973. Its main equipment was three CV-440s which it used to fly to Tobago. Other equipment was Beech 99. The airline ceased operations in 1974 and its main route was taken over by TTAS.

One of its three CV-440s in Port of Spain shortly before it went bankrupt. Photo taken in January 1974.

CAYMAN AIRWAYS (VR-C)

This company was formed in 1968 by the local government when it purchased 51 per cent of Cayman Brac Airways and reorganized it as Cayman Airways. Services began with a BAC-111 leased from LACSA. During the 1970s Cayman Airways used mainly BAC-111s until replaced by two ex-Air Florida B727-227s in 1982. For local services Cayman purchased a single SD-330 but it did not last long and was soon sold. The B727s gave away to leased new B737s in 1989 of which they currently operate four (two -200s and two -400s). The airline is still owned by the Cayman Government and carried 380,000 passengers in 1991. Cayman Airways serves five US cities (Miami, Atlanta, Houston, Tampa and New York). It plans to add Baltimore. For local services it sub-charters a BN Islander.

Sporting its new livery the B737-400 VR-CAA is seen approaching Miami in March 1992. It features the "Sir Turtle" logo on the fin which also represents the Cayman Islands.

CROWN AIR

Also known as "Dorado Wings", this local passenger airline in Puerto Rico became the biggest local carrier after Prinair's demise. Its fleet consisted of Twin Otters and BN2A Islander aircraft. However its domination was shortlived, with increased competition it finally ceased operations in March 1989.

One of Crownair's Twin Otters at San Juan, March 1986. Its aircraft rarely carried any titles.

CUBANA DE AVIACION

The present Cubana began operations in June 1961 as a successor to the original Compania Cubana de Aviacion (founded 1929). Throughout its history it has mainly used Russian equipment, such as Il-62, Tu-154, Il-18, An-26, An-24 and Yak-40. Prohibited from flying to USA, it mainly serves European destinations as well as Mexico City, Managua, Lima and Kingston amongst other local cities. It also operates an extensive domestic network.

Cubana currently operates two Il-76s, thirteen Il-62s, eight Tu-154s, twenty-six An-26s, twelve An-24s, ten Yak-40s plus various light aircraft and helicopters.

One of Cubana's Tu-154s rolling out for take off at Mexico City in October 1992.

DOMINICANA DE AVIACION

This international air carrier in the Dominican Republic was founded in 1944, again with Pan American assistance, and holding 40 per cent of the initial shares. Initial equipment was a Ford Trimotor leased from Cubana. Pan Am sold its shares in 1957 and the airline became locally owned.

It acquired two DC-4s in 1958 followed by two DC-6s in the early 1960s. After initially deciding for the BAC-111, Dominicana introduced a DC-9-32 in 1969, however the following year it crashed and was never replaced. For cargo operations, it purchased two Carvairs which remained in service well into the 1970s.

Dominicana began its long association with the B-727 in 1972. It quickly build up a fleet of one -100 and two -200 models. In the 1980s more B-727s were added along with a single B-707 which has now been withdrawn from service. For cargo services, Dominicana continued to rely on DC-6s, the last being added in 1977 with two continuing in service until the end of the 1980s. Mention should also be made of aircraft on short term leases such as the B-747 and A-300, none of which remain.

Lately Dominicana has introduced a metallic livery retaining the blue-red cheatline, as shown on its latest B-727-200, taken in Santo Domingo, November 1992.

Its livery has mostly consisted of a red and blue cheatline with white top as shown on its B-707 when in Miami, February 1986.

EXECUTIVE AIR

This local airline began on a small-scale in 1979 with a scheduled passenger service from San Juan to the US Virgin islands. It initially used light aircraft but by mid-1980s had moved up to two DH Herons. However the big step came in 1988 when the company was purchased by AMR and turned into the local American Eagle carrier. The Herons were quickly replaced by C-212s and ATR-42s and the network expanded. Today they totally dominate local passenger services out of San Juan, with a fleet of eight SD-360s, eight ATR-42s and two ATR-72s.

One of Executive Air's current ATR-42s climbing out from St. Kitts, March 1992.

FOUR STAR AIR CARGO

A newcomer to the cargo scene in Puerto Rico, Four Star has grown to five DC-3s since its start in 1982. Its headquarters are in St. Thomas, but it mostly flies out of San Juan. A single Cessna 402 is used for executive transports.

Two of Four Star's DC-3s lined up at a wet ramp in San Juan, November 1992.

HAITI TRANS AIR

This scheduled passenger airline based in Port-au-Prince was founded in 1986. For the most part of its existence it has relied on a single B727-200 leased from Peru, but it recently leased a DC-8-61 from the same source.

Haiti Trans Air's single B727 coming in to land in Miami, its main destination. It is still registered in Peru.

HELENAIR

This air-taxi company was set up in St. Lucia 1987, with its main equipment being the BN2A Islander.

One of Helenair's Islanders at Grenada, July 1992.

HISPANIOLA AIRWAYS

Named after the island of the Dominican Republic and Haiti, this airline operated cargo operations with a B707 aircraft until it ceased operations around 1984

Its B-707 in the process of being broken up at Miami in February 1986.

LIAT

LIAT, or Leeward Island Air Transport, as its full name reads, was set up in 1956 to provide an air service to the many smaller islands in the Leewards chain. BWIA provided an initial 51 per cent of the capital, and the local islands the remaining 49 per cent. Initial equipment consisted of light aircraft, but in 1965 LIAT began an association with the HS 748 which would last until the present time, although it replaced the original ones with new 748-2Bs in 1984-85. At the same time it also introduced DHC-8-100s on favourable terms offered by the Canadian government, who also assisted in building a hangar at Antigua.

In 1971 Court Line purchased BWIAs 75 per cent share of LIAT. When Court Line went bankrupt in 1974 LIAT ceased operations on the 15th August of the same year. The airline was taken over by the local governments, and restarted in September 1974 as LIAT(1974) Ltd. During Court Line's control it briefly operated BAC-111s, otherwise 748s and Twin Otters

had been its main equipment, with BN Islanders used for services to the smaller communities. Its network stretches from Caracas, Port of Spain and Georgetown in the south, up the chain to San Juan and the Dominican Republic in the north. The airline's main base its Antigua, but currently all its 748s with crews are based in Barbados.

V2-LAA is one of the original 748-2s which was delivered to LIAT in 1969 and traded back to Bae for new 748-2Bs in 1984-85. It is photographed at Port of Spain in October 1984.

V2-LDU is one of eight DHC-8-100s operated by LIAT. It is seen just about to take off from St. Maarten, February 1992.

NORTH CAY AIRWAYS

North Cay Airways was formed in 1970 to provide an air service from San Juan to the US Virgin Islands. In 1973 it became a subsidiary of Airways Enterprises Inc. Its main equipment was a large fleet of DC-3s, at least eleven were employed. North Cay ceased operations in 1976.

One of several North Cay DC-3s withdrawn from use at San Juan airport, November 1985. They were all later scrapped.

OCEANAIR

Oceanair was founded in 1978 to operate a scheduled air service from San Juan to mainly the US Virgin Islands. Initially it was known as "Trans Commuter Airline" and it began operations with Beech Queen Airs. It later introduced three F-27s and four CASA 212s before it ceased operations in August 1984.

After its demise its F-27s were stored at San Juan. N4302F was photographed in September 1985.

PRINAIR

Once the biggest regional airline in the USA with over a million passengers a year, it became a well-known company throughout the Caribbean. At its height it operated twenty-five Lycoming-powered Herons from its base at San Juan. It briefly introduced CASA 212s and CV-580s before Prinair went bankrupt in july 1985. It even had an order for CN-235s. During most of its history its Herons were painted in different colours, but towards the end it introduced a standard livery.

One of Prinair's many Herons, this was one of the very few to be repainted in the new livery. It is seen in San Juan shortly after the bankruptcy, November 1985.

SAINT LUCIA AIRWAYS

Saint Lucia Airways was founded in 1975 as a private airline for passenger and cargo services. An Islander was used for a shuttle service between Vigie and Hewannora airports in St. Lucia. During the mid-1980s it operated a C-130 Hercules and various B-707s plus Twin Otters on local flights. However in 1987 it suspended operations. Some media reports indicated that the airline operated on behalf of the CIA, mainly in Africa.

Its single C-130 during a visit to Miami, April 1986.
(E. Gual/Aviation Photography of Miami)

SAP

Servicios Aereos Profesionales in the Dominican Republic provides a scheduled domestic passenger service from the downtown airport in Santo Domingo. It currently uses two Twin Otters, but has also used light aircraft as well as a DH Heron for these routes.

One of SAPs' Twin Otters taxies out for take off at Herrera airport in Santo Domingo.

SOUTHERN FLYER

This all-cargo airline in Puerto Rico used three DC-3s during the 1980s from its base in San Juan. However, it currently only flies one of the aircraft.

One of Southern Flyer's DC-3s in San Juan, November 1985.

TAINO AIR

This small air-taxi company in the Bahamas was originally known as Lucaya Air but changed its name in 1987. It has operated various light aircraft from its base in Freeport for many years. Recently it has introduced a couple of E-110 Bandeirantes on scheduled regional routes.

One of Taino Air's Bandeirantes at Miami, July 1992.

TOL-AIR

This all-cargo airline in Puerto Rico has become a major operator out of San Juan with two CV-240s, five DC-3s, a Metro and various light aircraft. Its main activity is flying mail. The airline is owned by Cesar Toledo and was founded in 1983.

Its two CV-240s (or rather T-29s as they are ex-USAF) carry "Dodita" titles, the rest of the fleet carries "Tol-Air" titles. N357T was photographed in November 1992 in San Juan.

TRADO

Trans Dominican Airways, as its full name reads, began operating heavy cargo aircraft from Santo Domingo in the early 1980s. It briefly used a Constellation before switching to DC-6s and later a single DC-7. Both its DC-6s are now stored in Santo Domingo and the airline seems to rely mostly on its DC-7 for the cargo runs, with a single CV-440 used for *ad hoc* charter work. The CV-440 is painted in full TRADO livery, while the cargo aircraft are all operated in all-metallic, mostly without any titles.

TRADOs' single DC-7CF comes in for landing at Miami, July 1992. TRADO is one of the very last operators of DC-7 aircraft.

TRANS-JAMAICA AIRLINES

This regional airline in Jamaica was set up in 1975 as Jamaica Air Taxi with single-engined Cessnas and BN2A Islanders. It soon changed name to its current Trans-Jamaica. By 1980 it had introduced Trislanders on its domestic network. Its main base is the downtown airport of Kingston, and from here it flies to Montego Bay, Ocho Rios, Negril and Port Antonio. In the early 1980s it briefly operated a single DC-3 otherwise Islanders and Trislanders have been its equipment. In 1992 Trans-Jamaica leased two ex-Midway Do-228s, followed by an ATR-42 in 1993.

One of its Trislanders at Kingston's downtown airport, November 1985.

TROPICAL AIR SERVICE

Tropical Air Service was founded in 1973 to fly non-scheduled services in the Eastern Caribbean from its base in Barbados. Its main equipment was DC-3s, BN Islanders and some Shrike Commanders. In 1979 the airline was taken over by Air Dale of Canada. By the late 1980s it had ceased operations.

One of its DC-3s at Grantley Adams International airport, Barbados, January 1974. This particular DC-3 was destroyed in the Bahamas in July 1979 during the filming of the film "The Island".

TTAS

Trinidad and Tobago Air Service was set up in June 1974 after Caribbean United ceased operations. It was founded by the Trinidad & Tobago government to provide a scheduled passenger service between Trinidad and Tobago. Initial equipment was two DC-6s, but these were replaced by six new Bae.748s from 1977 to 1979. The airline was merged with BWIA in January 1980, but the 748s continued to fly mainly on the air-bridge between Port of Spain and Tobago, although they were also employed on routes to Grenada, St. Lucia and Martinique. Aircraft were also leased out to LIAT. All the 748s were phased out during 1986-87.

One of the ex-TTAS 748s at Beef Island, Tortola in November 1985. It still carries the basic TTAS livery minus the titles.

WINAIR

Windward Islands Airways was set up in August 1961 by local businessmen to operate a scheduled passenger service from St. Maarten to neighbouring islands using a Piper Apache. It later added other light aircraft such as a Dornier 28, and Beech Bonanza, until it stepped up to the Twin Otter in 1967. The airline was taken over by the Netherlands Antilles government in 1974 after it attempted to operate FH-227s to San Juan and almost went bankrupt. A second Twin Otter arrived in 1970, but these have since been replaced by three new DHC-6-300 Twin Otters which make up its current fleet. It briefly experimented with a single YS-11 but again it proved a financial drain on the airline and it was quickly grounded. Winair carries about 150,000 passengers a year and serves seven local destinations from its base at St. Maarten.

One of its Twin Otters coming in to land at St. Maarten, February 1992.

CENTRAL AMERICA

AERO COSTA RICA

This scheduled passenger airline was founded by some ex-Lacsa employees in Costa Rica. It began operations to Miami during the summer of 1992 with two leased ex-Pan Am B727-200s. However, the 727s turned out to be too large, hence they were soon replaced by two leased B737-200s.

One of Aero Costa Rica's B727s coming in to land in Miami, July 1992 shortly after the airline began operations. Notice it still carries the old Pan Am registration.

AEROPERLAS

This private domestic airline in Panama was founded in 1970, initially operating light aircraft. By the late 1970s its fleet stabilized around the DH Twin Otter. It operates from the down-town "Paitilla" airport in Panama City, and mainly flies to Colon on the Caribbean coast. It continues to· rely on the Twin Otter, and currently operates four.

One of Aeroperlas' Twin Otters taxies in to the terminal at Paitilla airport, February 1985.

AEROQUETZAL

Aeroquetzal began operations in the late 1980s with a single CV-580, mainly flying from its base at Guatemala City to Flores. It soon replaced the CV-580 with a DC-9-15 but the airline went bankrupt during spring 1992, and its DC-9 was returned.

Its single CV-580 TG-MYM which was soon replaced by a DC-9. (Aerogem)

AEROVIAS CARIARI

This domestic airline in Costa Rica began operations in 1968 from its base in Limon. Its main equipment was DC-3s but it also employed a CV-440 and light aircraft. By the late 1970s it suspended operations.

One of Aerovias Cariari's DC-3s at San Jose in 1978. (D. Hagedorn)

AEROVIAS SA

This mainly domestic airline in Guatemala began operations in 1977 with small aircraft. In 1984 it acquired the first of three HP Heralds, one of which is still in service. It has also leased aircraft as required such as Caravelle and B-727s. It is about to add a B-737-200 to its fleet.

Its main activity is a daily flight from Guatemala City to Flores, famous for its Maya ruins named "Tikal", but it also flies to Chetumal in Mexico and Belize. Aerovias holds traffic rights for Miami.

One of Aerovias' stored Heralds at Guatemala City, October 1992. One Herald remains in service.

AESA

Aerolineas el Salvador SA operated a couple of DC-6s on cargo operations during the 1970s and 1980s

One of its DC-6s, YS-03C, seen in 1979, was acquired by AESA in 1975. (D. Hagedorn)

AIR PANAMA

Air Panama was set up in 1966 to replace previous local airlines which had ceased operations. Iberia initially held 49 per cent of the shares. First equipment was a DC-9, and it soon expanded a network from Panama to Guayaquil, Lima, Miami, Mexico City and Guatemala. B-727-100s soon replaced the DC-9 and this became the main equipment until the demise of the airline. However a DC-10 was leased for a short time from Jet 24 for the Miami route.

Iberia withdrew its share in 1978.

In the aftermath of the US invasion of Panama, the airline entered economic difficulties and ceased operations in January 1990. Its assets were purchased in July 1991 by a private group that called themselves "Panama Air International" with the intention of restarting operations during 1992, however this has not yet happened.

One of Air Panama´s B727s during a scheduled stop at Guayaquil, Ecuador in September 1985.

APSA

Aerovias Puntarenas SA was founded in 1961 to fly domestic services to the western part of Costa Rica, around Puntarenas. Amongst its types employed were DC-3, C-46 and CV-440. It ceased operations in 1978 and its routes were taken over by SANSA.

APSAs' single C-46 caught in San Jose in the mid-1970s. (D. Hagedorn)

AVIATECA

This national airline of Guatemala began operations in 1948, mainly on domestic routes. The government was the sole shareholder. In 1955 it opened a route to New Orleans, after that followed Miami, Mexico City and San Salvador. Initial equipment was, as always, DC-3s but also such unusual aircraft as the Northrop YC-125 and Fairchild C-82 saw service with Aviateca. Jet operations began in 1974 with BAC-111, and like its sister airline in Honduras, Aviateca introduced CV-440s on domestic services, later replaced by F-27s.

Today Aviateca is an all-jet operator with a fleet of B-737-200 & 300s. TACA has taken a minority shareholding in Aviateca as well, and the two airlines now interchange aircraft and coordinate its activities, as part of the TACA group.

The B727-100 was the backbone of Aviateca´s equipment during the 1980s when it operated two. TG-ALA was caught in Miami, September 1985. The livery by this time was rather simple, as opposed to the very colourful yellow-orange livery used in the 1970s.

AVIONES DE PANAMA

This small non-scheduled air-taxi company was founded in 1964. It has always flown light aircraft, mainly BN Islanders and Trislanders from its base at Paitilla airport. By 1988 it had disappeared from the scene.

One of its BN Trislanders at Paitilla airport in February 1985.

CHITREANA DE AVIACION

This small domestic airline in Panama operated two DC-3s on local services during the late 1970s and most of the 1980s. Its roots actually go back to 1952 when it began operations with a Stinson V-77. In recent years the DC-3s have been replaced by a BN Trislander. As its name implies, the airline is based in Chitre, Panama.

One of its DC-3s caught in 1977.
(D. Hagedorn)

COPA

This international airline in Panama was founded in 1944 by the local government and Pan Am, services beginning in 1947 with DC-3s on domestic routes. During the 1960s COPA gradually expanded its network in Central America, and introduced HS 748 in 1966. Pan Am withdrew its interest in COPA in 1971, and in the same year COPA added an L.Electra to its fleet. With its lower operating cost on short routes COPA could offer low fares. The DC-3s stayed in the fleet until 1980 while the Electra was gone a couple of years later. By now COPA relied on the B-737 as its main and only equipment. With the demise of Air Panama, COPA has been able to expand its network and fleet, it now serves Central America, the Caribbean and the US with four B-737s

COPA's colourful livery as shown on this B-737 on approach to Miami airport in May 1992.

One of Exaco's two DC-6s. (D. Hagedorn)

EXACO CARGO

This all-cargo airline in Costa Rica began on a small scale in 1956 and then gradually grew until it flew a couple of DC-6s in the late 1970s, however in 1980 it suspended operations.

INAIR PANAMA

This all-cargo airline in Panama was founded in 1967 and began operations with C-46s, initially to Central and South America. In 1969 it received permission to serve Miami. During the 1970s it relied mainly on DC-6s, with its fleet reaching four aircraft in 1976. In the early 1980s it leased various jet aircraft such as CV-880s and DC-8s, however by 1987 it had ceased operations.

One of Inair's DC-6s caught at Miami in 1978. (D. Hagedorn)

ISLEÑA AIRLINES

This regional airline based in La Ceiba, Honduras began operations in 1982. It flies a scheduled domestic air service, and has recently begun services to the Cayman Islands. Its equipment has varied, from Twin Otters, Bandeirantes to G-1 and F-27. Recently Isleña has incorporated two SD-360s.

Isleña's G-1 pictured at the Cayman Islands, March 1992, about to return on its regular flight from La Ceiba. The G-1 has since been sold in Guatemala.

LACSA

Lineas Aereas Costarricense SA was founded in 1945 with a leased DC-3. In 1954 it became the first airline in the region to introduce CV-340s. In 1955 a subsidiary was set up on the Cayman Islands. This later led to extensive cooperation with Cayman Airways. DC-6s were introduced in 1961, and the first jet aircraft, BAC-111, followed in 1967.

Later when SANSA was established as the domestic airline of Costa Rica, Lacsa became a majority shareholder.

As with several other Central American airlines, Pan Am had a shareholding of 40 per cent in Lacsa when it was set up, and this was not sold until 1970. During the

1970s Lacsa's main equipment was the BAC-111 but some C-46s and DC-6s remained in the fleet, as did some Electras for all-cargo work in the later part of the 1970s. The first B-727-200s arrived in 1980 and eventually replaced all BAC-111s. A single DC-8 was used for all-cargo work, while the B-727 became the backbone of the fleet in the 1980s. However, in December 1990, the first two of five A320s

arrived to start replacing the B727s. Lacsa also ordered two A-310s but these were cancelled in 1992. TACA purchased a minority shareholding in Lacsa and Lacsa now coordinates its schedule with them.

Its latest type is the A320, N481GX leased from GATX, and about to touch down in Miami, May 1992.

LANICA

"Lineas Aereas de Nicaragua" was set up as an affiliate of Pan Am in 1944, scheduled services beginning two years later with Boeing 247s and DC-3s. In 1950 it took over another local airline named FANSA. Lanica began operations to Miami in December 1957 and at the same time ordered Viscounts, however these were soon sold due to financial problems being experienced. The DC-6 continued to be its main equipment on international routes until replaced by BAC-111s in the mid-1960s. By this time the airline was controlled by the Somoza family although Pan Am maintained an interest (it was sold in August 1974).

Lanica leased a pair of CV-880s in 1972 soon followed by two more. However, C-46s and DC-6s continued to fly domestic and cargo services during the 1970s, while the CV-880s were replaced by B-727 by the end of the decade.

The overthrow of the Somoza regime in 1979 almost grounded the airline but it continued at a much reduced scale with C-46s until it was disbanded in 1981.

Instead a new airline was founded by the new Sandinista regime in November 1980, called *Aeronica*. Even the national ICAO abbreviation for Nicaragua was changed from "AN-" to "YN-". Two C-212s were incorporated for the domestic network, while C-46s, DC-3s and DC-6s still operated on domestic and cargo routes well into the 1980s. With closer relations with the then Soviet Union, Aeronica added AN-32s for the domestic network and a single Tu-154 for its international services (in addition to the B-727 and B-720 already used). However, the continuing economic problems seriously affected Aeronica. Hence with the newly-elected Chamorra government, the airline was privatized and renamed again. Now

Aeronica introduced a new bold livery, as shown on its single B727-100 during one of its frequent visits to Miami.
(E. Gual/Aviation Photography of Miami)

simply known as *Nica* it began operations as such in 1992. TACA assumed an interest in the airline thus linking all Central American airlines together except for COPA in Panama.

SAHSA

Servicio Aereos de Honduras SA is the national airline of Honduras and was founded in November 1944. Initial equipment was the DC-3. In 1953 it acquired TACA of Honduras and four years later it purchased ANSHA. Having been a major shareholder since the beginning, Pan Am sold its 38 per cent share to TAN in 1970. TAN itself was completely absorbed by SAHSA in 1991. In the same year the government sold its 40 per cent share to TACA of Salvador, the balance being owned by local business interests.

Fleet-wise it relied on the DC-3 until the late 1950s when C-46s were introduced, followed by CV-440s in the late 1960s. The Electra first arrived in 1969. The first B-737 arrived in 1974, and by late 1992 SAHSA operated five B-737-200s plus a single DC-3 retained for *ad hoc* charter. In January 1994 SAHSA was forced to suspend operations due to insurance problems. TACA took over most of its international routes.

SAHSA's last operational DC-3 has recently been completely refurbished and is in immaculate condition. It was used for ad hoc charters. Picture taken in Tegucigalpa, October 1992.

SERCA

This all-cargo airline in Costa Rica operated initially leased DC-8s but later its own CV-880 on all-cargo flights in the early 1980s. However it subsequently went bankrupt and its CV-880 was stored for many years at Caracas International airport.

SERCA's CV-880, named "The Bullet", seen stored at Maiquetia airport outside Caracas, September 1989.

SETCO

SETCO flies two DC-3s and a couple of Aerocommanders on semi-regular flights from Tegucigalpa, Honduras. Its name stands for "Servicios Ejecutivos Turisticos Commander" and it has been operating since the early 1980s.

One of SETCO's two DC-3s caught at Tegucigalpa, October 1992.

TACA

TACA of El Salvador can trace its history back to 1932 when it began operations with one aircraft on one route. It was set up by Lowell Yerex. He built up this airline to a major international carrier by the 1940s serving 235 points in sixteen countries, from Miami to Rio de Janeiro. TACA set up subsidiary airlines in Guatemala, Nicaragua, Costa Rica, Honduras, Brazil (Empr Tr.Aerovias Brazil), Mexico, Venezuela, Colombia and Trinidad (BWIA). All were controlled through a holding company, TACA Airways which was set up in Panama in 1939. The fleet in 1940 consisted of forty-six aircraft of which twenty-six were Ford Trimotors. In that year it flew 65,000 passengers, which grew to 90,000 the following year.

In October 1940, American Export Lines Inc bought a controlling interest in TACA which then became a US airline. To respond to its growing dominance, Pan Am set up a new subsidiary in Guatemala (which later became Aviateca) to compete with TACA. Following this TACA de Guatemala soon lost its licence. Later American Export was forced to sell its share in TACA. However, TWA stepped in and bought a large interest in October 1943. TACA's network peaked in 1946. However, by now, Pan Am set up a string of subsidiaries to compete with TACA, such as Avensa in Venezuela, Bahamas Airways, Dominicana de Aviacion, COPA in Panama, LACSA, SAHSA and Lanica. TACA's operation began to fall apart, during the spring of 1948 they sold all Central American subsidiaries except those in El Salvador. Colombia and Brazil had been sold off earlier. In May 1951

TACA transferred its official base from Panama to New Orleans, with the Waterman Steamship Corp becoming the biggest shareholder, after it bought TWAs shares. TACA went through various ownership changes during the 1950s, but in 1964 Ricardo Kriete purchased 32 per cent, with the remainder being in the hands of US interests. In 1966 TACA became the first airline in Central America to introduce the BAC-111, having earlier acquired Viscounts. These along with some DC-6s remained in service until mid-1978 when the first of many B-737s

TACA's B-737 taking on passengers in El Salvador, February 1985. It features the current livery.

arrived. L-188 had then replaced the DC-6s as freighters. The first B-767 arrived in 1985.

In the last few years TACA has purchased substantial interests in Aviateca, SAHSA, LACSA, *Nica* and is working closely with COPA, thus almost repeating the pattern of the 1940s. Its fleet consists of eight B-737s and two B-767s.

TAN

Transportes Aereas Nacionales was founded in Honduras in 1945 and for many years operated in competition with the other Honduran airline, SAHSA. However, in 1970 TAN bought Pan Am's shares, and the two airlines started cooperating although still flying under separate names. In 1991 they were completely merged under the SAHSA name.

TAN used mainly C-46s, DC-6s, DC-7s, L.Electras and B-737s during its history. The B-737 was introduced in 1974.

This B-737-200 HR-TNR became TANs' first jet equipment in 1974. It was originally delivered to PLUNA of Uruguay.
(E. Gual/Aviation Photography of Miami)

MEXICO

AERO CALIFORNIA

As its name indicates, it operates from Baja California to many domestic points in Mexico and Los Angeles. It was founded in 1960 in La Paz, Baja California, and its main owners are the Arechiga family. For many years it operated a small fleet of light aircraft plus DC-3s and CV-340s. It introduced a single DC-9-15 in 1982 and this became its main aircraft until Mexico deregulated. It then expanded rapidly and now operates nine of these DC-9s on a network that mainly covers the north-western part of Mexico and to California.

One of Aero California's colourful DC-9s at Mexico City, November 1992.

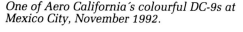

AERO CARIBE/COZUMEL

These two regional airlines, based in Cancun, began operations during the mid-1970s. AeroCozumel mainly flew between Cancun and Cozumel island, while Aero Caribe flew throughout the Yucatan peninsula. Initial equipment was BN Islanders and CV-440s, but they were later substituted by F-27s and FH-227s.

Both airlines were operated as two separate entities but under the same ownership. However, Mexicana purchased both airlines and reorganized them as "Mexicana Inter". At the same time a new division was set up in Monterrey as "Aero Monterrey". Mexicana bought eight FH-227s from Britt in the USA, to add to the fleet. The aircraft are currently being repainted in a modified Mexicana livery.

Aero Caribe's FH-227 at Oaxaca, July 1988.

AEROESLAVA

This long-time overhaul company based in Mexico City acquired heavy aircraft in 1992. Apart from a single DC-3 and F-27, it purchased a couple of Viscount 700s in the USA. These are used for cargo and *ad hoc* charter work.

Aeroeslava's Viscount in Mexico City, July 1992. It carries the basic livery of the previous owner.

AERO GUADALAJARA

This regional airline based in Guadalajara began operations during spring 1991 with Gulfstream G-1. With two of these twenty-four seaters, it served Monterrey, Tampico, San Luis de Potosi and Pto Vallarta with scheduled services. It is owned by two families whose main business is the trucking business. However, in 1993 it ceased scheduled services and became a charter company.

Aero Guadalajara's G-1 at its home base in August 1992.

AEROLITORAL

This regional airline based in Monterrey was founded in 1989 simply as "Litoral". It acquired four YS-11s and began a local service. However it was soon purchased by Aeromexico and renamed Aerolitoral. The YS-11s were phased out, and instead Aerolitoral ordered twenty-seven new Metro IIIs. Some of these are used by the other feeder airline, called Aeroponiente, in Guadalajara.

The Metros now sport a livery similar to the one used by the current Aeromexico. This Metro was photographed at its base in Monterrey, August, 1992.

AEROMAR

This private regional airline is based in Mexico City and was founded in 1987. It serves a number of communities with its fleet of four ATR-42s.

Aeromar's ATR-42 caught in Zihuatanejo, July 1988.

AEROMEXICO

This international airline of Mexico was for many years state-owned and known as Aeronaves de Mexico. It began on a small scale in the mid-1930s by taking over some small privately owned Mexican domestic airlines. In September 1940 Pan Am acquired 40 per cent of the airline and immediately upgraded the fleet with Boeing 247s and DC-2s. Aeronaves continued its process of taking over small independent carriers and thus expanding its network. After increasing its capital in 1946, Aeronaves could introduce its first DC-3s to be followed by the first DC-4s in 1949.

Aeronaves went through a drastic change in 1952 when it took over LAMSA from United and Aerovias Reforma in the following year. Aeronaves now had an impressive domestic network. At the same time it added CV-240s. The competition with Mexicana increased which added pressure to acquire modern aircraft. After leasing a couple of Constellations, Aeronaves ordered two B.Britannias in 1957, and these were soon put on the New York route. After Pan Am pulled out, and a strike began, the airline was nationalized in July 1959. Aeronaves quickly bought six DC-6s from SAS to replace older

After it was reorganized under private ownership, Aeromexico introduced a blue-red livery, as seen on this B-767 about to land in Miami, March 1992.

equipment and introduced its first DC-8 in 1960. Aeronaves also took over Aerovias Guest's network in 1962 after Guest collapsed. The early 1960s saw a gradual increase of the network in the US and Europe. For the local routes, Aeronaves introduced DC-9s in 1967. Aeronaves formed a network of feeder airlines in 1968 under the "Aeronaves Alimentadora" name, equipment used was Twin Otters and HS.748s.

On 28th January, 1972 Aeronaves changed its name to simply "Aeromexico", and introduced a new livery. At the same time it ordered its first two DC-10s. In 1979 Aeromexico ordered its first MD-80s.

AERO SUDPACIFICO

This small family-owned regional airline is based in Uruapan. With three Metro IIs it flies a regional scheduled air service. It also undertakes charter flights. Apart from three Metros, Aero Sudpacifico also flies a BN Islander.

Aero Sudpacifico's Metro at Mexico City, which it serves from Uruapan, March 1992.

AEROVIAS OAXAQUEÑAS

One of many small feeder airlines, Aerovias Oaxaqueñas flew DC-3s from Oaxaca during the 1980s. It briefly introduced a leased F-27 before it went bankrupt.

This DC-3 was photographed in Oaxaca, July 1988.

AVIACSA

This scheduled passenger airline was set up to provide services from Tuxtla Gutierrez down-town airport to mainly Mexico City. It began operations with leased Bae.146s, but then switched to four F-100s leased from GPA. It now flies to various locations on the Yucatan peninsula, as well as Mexico City and Monterrey.

One of Aviacsa's F-100s caught in Merida, May 1992.

ESTRELLAS DEL AIRE

This small non-scheduled airline began operations in 1992 with a single DC-9-14. The airline is part of the large Estrellas del Oro bus company. Its DC-9 operates both charters and cargo flights from its base in Mexico City.

Estrellas' DC-9 preparing for take off at Mexico City's airport, November 1992.

MAYA CARGA

This small all-cargo airline flew a single DC-6 from its base at Merida in the late 1980s. However it later ceased operations, and its DC-6 is currently stored in Florida.

Maya Carga's DC-6 being stored at Tamiami airport, July 1992.

MEXICANA

Mexicana is one of the oldest surviving airlines in Latin America. It was founded in August 1924 and began scheduled operations two years later. The first route was Mexico City-Tuxpan-Tampico. During the 1920s it gradually increased its domestic network along the eastern coastline. Pan American purchased the airline in January 1929, and began a process of acquiring shares in airlines in most Latin American countries. By the end of the 1930s Mexicana served most of the important cities in Mexico from its base in the capital. It had also introduced modern equipment, namely Lockheed Electras and Boeing 247s. In May 1937 the first DC-2 was introduced.

In 1946 Pan American reduced its shareholding to 41 per cent, and in the same year supplied Mexicana with its first DC-4s. The first DC-6s followed four years later. In the 1950s Mexicana increased its presence on the US market by launching services to San Antonio and Chicago in 1957 with its new DC-7Cs. It already served Los Angeles.

Mexicana introduced its first jets in 1960, when it began flying three new DH Comets, and new US destinations added such as Dallas in 1961. The Comet was followed by an order for four B-727s in 1965, and thus Mexicana began an association with this trijet that would last close to 30 years, as Mexicana has only

For many years Mexicana used a gold livery with black titles as shown on this DC-10-15 preparing for take off at Mexico City International Airport in November 1992.

recently started to phase out this workhorse. However in the early 1960s the losses increased and Pan Am´s remaining shareholding was taken over by C. Ballesteros in 1967. A new management team turned the airline around. By 1977 Mexicana had grown to become the biggest airline in Latin America. It then had a fleet of twenty B-727-100/200s. The following year it carried five million passengers for the first time in a year. In September 1979 it ordered two DC-10-15s, a special version developed for Mexico. Again Mexicana entered a period of losses which culminated in the take-over of the airline by the Mexican government in July 1982, when it acquired 58 per cent. Since then it has been privatized and is now controlled by the same owner as Aeromexico.

NOROESTE

This regional airline based in Hermosillo was founded in 1988. It began operations with two leased F-27s, but they were soon replaced by a couple of ATR-42s. For a new route, linking Hermosillo with Mexico City, Noroeste leased a B737-500 from GPA in 1992. At the same time it transferred its ATR-42s to TAESA, leaving just a single 737 in its fleet.

Noroeste's single B737 about to take off in Mexico City, October 1992.

SARO

SARO, or Servicios Aereos Rutas Oriente, as its full name reads, was founded in 1991, to provide a scheduled air service from Monterrey. It first began with a single BAC-111, but this was soon replaced by three B737s, later supplemented by a B727-100. SARO recently purchased two B727-200s from Mexicana, as well as leasing two DC-9-30s.

SARO flies various domestic trunk routes from its base at Monterrey. The airline is owned by local business interests in Monterrey.

One of SARO's B737s in Monterrey, August, 1992.

TAESA

Transportes Aereos Ejecutivos SA began as an air-taxi operator in 1987 in Mexico City. It built up a large fleet of Learjets and L.Jetstars. TAESA constructed a large hangar and maintenance base at Mexico City's international airport.

With the deregulation of domestic aviation in Mexico, TAESA soon launched an ambitious drive into scheduled passenger services. It began on a small-scale with a couple of B727s flying couriers, but quickly built up a large fleet of these trijets for domestic passenger service and international charter business. The B727s were soon supplemented by leased B737s, B757s and a single B767 from GPA. TAESA launched charter services to Europe with its B757 and B767. In 1992 TAESA took over La Tur after its bankruptcy. Its A300 was returned but the MD-87s were incorporated into the TAESA fleet. With the ATR-42s from Noroeste, TAESA launched a regional air service from Cancun, although recently the ATRs were put up for sale.

One of TAESA's many B727s at Merida, May, 1992. TAESA has since modified its livery, so now the fin is yellow.